GHOST RECON™

PRIMA'S OFFICIAL STRATEGY GUIDE

MICHAEL SEARLE

PRIMA GAMES
A DIVISION OF RANDOM HOUSE, INC.
3000 LAVA RIDGE COURT
ROSEVILLE, CA 95661
1-800-733-3000
WWW.PRIMAGAMES.COM

Associate Product Manager: Jill Hinckley

Project Editor: Michelle Trujillo

Editorial Assistant: Matt Sumpter

ISBN: 0-7615-4191-8

Library of Congress Catalog Card Number: 2002114732

Printed in the United States of America

02 03 04 05 GG 10 9 8 7 6 5 4 3 2 1

CONTENTS

INTRODUCTION

In Ghost Recon, the enemy hits hard with soldiers and tanks.

They are the Ghosts—unseen soldiers who move through the night, as silent as spirits. They are America's elite Special Forces team, sent to the world's political hotspots to keep the peace through whatever means possible. Against the *zing* of sniper fire or the *baboom* of tank artillery, the Ghosts risk life and limb for the greater good. You're about to join them.

Your soldiers are determined to get the job done, no matter the mission.

It's the year 2008, and an extremist group has seized power in Russia. The radicals are determined to restore communist Russia to its former glory, and they have the military might to make it happen. Without pretense, the radicals invade Ukraine, Belarus, and Kazakhstan. The U.S.-backed NATO responds with troops of its own.

For the more remote missions, helicopters drop you off at the insertion zone— then you're on your own.

Tension escalates, casualties mount, and U.S. leaders choose the only alternative to war—your team of Green Berets, the Ghosts. Your series of covert operations will decide the future of the entire region.

The Ghosts can blend into any terrain, striking like vipers.

No one knows their ranks. No one knows their names. When the Ghosts complete a mission, people never know it happened. With war on the horizon, they give us all a ghost of a chance.

BASIC TRAINING

It's just you and five other teammates. There is no army at your backs.

You don't have an army to back you up. If this were a regular military tour of duty, you could depend on several thousand troops or maybe a division of M1A2 Abrams tanks and heavy air support to help with your objectives. Not with the Ghosts. You're stuck with two teams of three operatives each. You'd better choose the right men for the job, or you're unlikely to penetrate the local bingo night undetected, let alone a Russian command post.

PERSONNEL FILES

In *Ghost Recon*, each soldier has four skills: Weapon, Stealth, Endurance, and Leadership. After each successful mission, participating operatives each receive a combat point to increase a skill. Spend these wisely, or you'll end up with a sniper who can take two shots to the chest but can't sneak up on a guard enjoying a siesta.

Spend your combat points on Weapon skill first so you can shoot straight.

RANKING THE STATS

The most important skill is Weapon. Weapon represents the soldier's accuracy with his gun, as well as how fast his reticle pips (crosshairs) close on a target. There's nothing more frustrating than picking off bad guys like Jesse James while your supporting teammates miss every shot. Equally annoying is when your soldier's crosshairs close slower than a rusted elevator door. Avoid this by spending combat points, whenever possible, on Weapon. A good rule of thumb is to spend two of every three combat points earned on the Weapon skill.

There's a difference in weapon accuracy. Notice how the rifleman's M16 reticle pips don't close as tightly as a sniper's rifle.

TIP
Spend two of every three combat points earned on your Weapon skill.

Next up is Stealth, which represents your skill at moving quietly and, therefore, how close you can get to an enemy without being detected. You always want to surprise your enemies, especially if you can get off several rounds before they can return fire, so stealth is a must. Avoid soldiers with a Stealth of one—the lowest Stealth number for a fireteam brings down the entire team's ability to sneak up on an enemy. If you have to take someone low in Stealth, spend the points early to bring him up to an acceptable two or three.

With a high Stealth, you can sneak up on an enemy and pick him off while he's tying his shoe. A low Stealth means patrols will spot you a mile away.

A high Leadership can be critical, though only one of your soldiers has to concentrate on it. For every three points, Leadership increases all other soldiers' skills by one. It's very important since it beefs up five of the six soldiers. However, only pump up one of your guys since the game checks the highest Leadership in the platoon and designates that soldier as the leader. The effect isn't cumulative, so having two operatives with a high Leadership is a waste, unless you want one as a backup in case the other kicks the bucket.

Without a high Endurance, the ability to sustain injury, you'll end up like these guys.

Endurance signifies the ability to withstand physical damage. A single shot takes out low-Endurance guys, but a soldier with an Endurance of eight can take a couple of wounds. Also, a soldier with a low Endurance can be slowed down in combat if he's carrying too much equipment. Endurance is the least important stat for two big reasons. First, missions are based on stealth; you should avoid heavy-duty firefights. Second, you can always restart a mission or return to a previously saved position if one of your men takes a bullet.

NOT ALL RECRUITS ARE THE SAME

Soldiers start with different skill points, from four to eight. Pay attention to the new recruits' points, and you'll see some are better than others. Some have seven points while others only have four points. Obviously, for the best fighting chance, you want a platoon full of seven-point operatives. Unfortunately, that's not possible; there just aren't enough high-stat studs to go around. A soldier is acceptable with six skill points, especially with high Weapon and Stealth numbers.

To improve your chances of a killer squad, try this trick. Look at your recruits, and if you're not happy with the result, simply restart the campaign. Each restart spawns new recruits, so you can keep going till you find the platoon you like.

TIP
If you're not happy with your platoon's beginning stats, restart the campaign and get a whole new set of recruits to choose from.

Don't worry if you can't find the ultimate set of six soldiers. As you complete missions, the game unlocks 12 different specialists (one after each of the first 12 missions) in the Ghost Recon campaign and five specialists (one after each of the first five missions) in the Desert Siege campaign. These specialists come ready to go with high stats and special weapons, so include them in the mix if you need their skills, replacing one soldier for another.

The rifleman has the best chance of survival in a close firefight.

THE ALPHA/BRAVO TAG TEAM

Every mission in *Ghost Recon* can be accomplished with just two teams. During times of particularly hairy gunfire, it's difficult to switch between characters and not end up like Swiss cheese. That said, the first slot of both Alpha and Bravo should be filled with a rifleman. When you're moving a fireteam on a mission, your rifleman will most likely engage the enemy first. If someone has to shoot from close to medium range, it should be your rifleman and his M16. A support soldier might get big casualties, but he'll also take a slug just as quickly, and a sniper's reload is just too slow for rapid-fire kills. In a quick fight, the rifleman has the best chance of survival.

Most of the time, either your Alpha or Bravo rifleman will also be your leader. Snipers need to raise their Weapon and Stealth skills faster since they're the ones crawling amidst the enemy patrols. Support and demolitions soldiers aren't guaranteed to come on every mission. That leaves riflemen with a few extra combat points to spend on Leadership.

You should take at least one demo expert on each mission. If you run into any tanks, you'll be glad you did.

The second slot for each fireteam rotates depending on the mission. You should always take at least one demolitions expert on every mission. There's always something to blow up, even if it's not scheduled in the mission. You might not need to plant a demo charge on a downed F18, but you can always aim an M136 Rocket Launcher at a group of hostiles and inflict heavy damage.

Support or another rifleman? You make the call, depending on whether you need additional firepower or a better all-around soldier.

If the demo expert goes into Alpha, your next choice for Bravo depends on your play style. A support soldier carries around the hefty M249 Machine Gun and rips through a lot of shells. If you're expecting heavy resistance and lots of firefights, bring along a support guy. Otherwise, they tend to be a bit trigger-happy and open up on anything that moves. That can prove troublesome and makes your whole fireteam a target. Usually, a third rifleman works better. He can give you some additional firepower with a quicker trigger and more mobility. Another option is a second demolitions soldier. Planning for the future is always good, and bringing two demo guys increases their combat value, so they're ready for the tougher missions.

CAUTION

Don't bring along dead weight on missions. Remember, you want your important soldiers to earn extra combat points—two snipers are an advantage.

Snipers are your best shots and your long-range vision.

The third slot in each fireteam is all about the sniper, the most important soldier in the game. This book's combat strategies constantly utilize the sniper's long-range scope for surveillance and mission planning. Snipers sit in the rear, mostly for protection. They aren't that effective in firefights, so your riflemen and support should be up closer in case of a sudden attack. Plus, when a fireteam is hunkered down, the sniper has the best range and can hit a target from the back position. Even though the sniper sits third, you'll find yourself controlling him more than any other in the unit.

CAUTION

Never auto assign your platoon. The computer doesn't look at stats wisely, and you may end up with a four-point loser in a critical slot.

BATTLE PREPARATIONS

You're not in the field yet. Before you jump hastily into a mission, you must remember a few things that don't rely on how fast you can press the trigger button. Here are some premission tips to get you ready for battle.

DON'T KEEP THE BRIEFING BRIEF

Pay attention during the mission briefing. It can tell you what sort of enemy you're up against and provide valuable clues to defeating your obstacles.

Pay attention during the mission briefing. First, it spells out your tasks on the mission, which are your top priorities. It also gives you clues about the type of resistance you'll face, as well as possible nasty surprises. For example, say you're deep in a mission without a demo soldier and his trusty M136. If you stumble across a tank, you're toast. Your men don't have the weaponry to deal with an armored vehicle without demolitions. You also shouldn't forget a demo charge on a mission with a demolitions target; otherwise, you will forfeit the mission objective or reward. Study your briefing to be better prepared for the task ahead.

SAVE YOURSELF

Ghost Recon can make you paranoid. If it's not the crunch of leaves right next to you, it's a guard who suddenly appears out of the trees. You can become incredibly frustrated if you don't "paranoid save" often. You should save after *every* major firefight. If you get killed after that point without saving, you will have to repeat the battle.

Beware of friendly fire. Never position one soldier directly in front of another.

No one should die in your team either. Some fans like to play *Ghost Recon* with no saves and if a soldier dies, a soldier dies. The game is hard enough without this added pressure. Once you become an expert, you can play that way. Until then, stick to saving so you can keep your team members alive and earning combat points each mission.

MOVEMENT

Most people think shooting is the key to a game like *Ghost Recon*. It's not. Stealthy movement and tactics keep you alive. It helps to kill the enemy in a single shot, but if you aren't in the proper position, the return fire can cut you to ribbons. Your missions will be much more successful if you move and deploy according to the following guidelines.

THE CROSSFIRE

Set up a crossfire and one of your men will always have a free blind-side shot at the enemy.

Use the cover provided on every mission, from trees in the forests to cars in the city streets.

Ideally, you spot the bad guys before they spot you and move into position. Team Alpha takes a position in cover near enough to draw an arc of fire on the unsuspecting enemies. Team Bravo does the same thing from the opposite side. One team opens up, and if any enemies survive the initial barrage, their attention is fixed on the first team. They don't have a chance against the wave of bullets hitting them from their unprotected side.

The idea here is to move one team a short distance, then have the first team cover the second team as it moves. As you work toward your objective, the teams flank out around the enemy. If one team runs into a group of hostiles, it doesn't have to fight alone. In fact, the other team should surprise the hostiles and take them down before they have a chance to mow down the vulnerable team. A team's arc of fire should always be straight ahead or aimed in front of the second team's planned location.

SNIPER TIME

The sniper's more than a really good shot. Each of your fireteams uses the sniper's telescopic sight for recon.

Use your sniper's telescopic sight to spot the enemy before he spots you.

TIP

Flanking your enemies assaults them with gunfire from two different directions. Even a fortified position can't hold long.

Here's an example of how to work together. Team Alpha wants to move into a cave entrance, but it's dark, and line of sight is nearly impossible to establish from the team's current position. If enemies are inside, they could be hidden in a crevice ready to blow someone's brains out. Move team Bravo into the trees nearby with an arc of fire into the cave. When team Alpha gives up its secured position and charges into the cave, Bravo has first shots at anyone foolish enough to pop up. There are no guarantees in dangerous situations like this, but getting the first shots often makes the difference.

Before you move a team's position, scout the surrounding area with the sniper. Move carefully until you spot an enemy at long range. Identify all the enemies in the area using both team's snipers, then plan a route that can flank the nearest ones without danger from return fire. If you can't engage an enemy without exposing your backs to other enemies, then use your sniper to pick off as many targets as possible, and relocate to attack from a different angle.

For example, say you want to take a ridge guarded by a fortified machine gun post atop the rocky cliffs. If you were to charge up the slope, guns blazing, the machine gunner would probably bury you before you got halfway up the hill. Instead, try zooming in with the sniper's scope and monitoring the post for a few minutes. First, you notice two guards up there; more importantly, you discover that the machine gunner leaves his weapon every so often to take a stroll. Time the raid for when the gunner next leaves, and have your sniper take out the second guard. With your second team charging up the hill, keep your sniper focused on the machine gun. You can't let that be manned, or your friends are doomed. The second someone grabs the machine gun, pick him off. A little luck will have you unscathed and inside the post in no time.

A sniper's rifle does more than shoot. It can also aid you in dodging fights you don't want to start.

CROUCHING SOLDIER, HIDDEN ENEMY

This is not a racing game. Speed through *Ghost Recon* and you'll alert every enemy unit and have a losing gunfight on your hands. You need to move slowly, using your snipers to note every enemy location and scout out the best spots to move under cover.

Never stand on a mission. Always crouch or crawl while moving to a destination.

Never stand during a mission. You move a little slower in the crouch position, and it increases your defense. Work your way from tree to rock, vehicle to building, as you search out your objectives. When you let the computer A.I. plan a route for your alternate team, always double-check to make sure the team is hidden in the best cover in the area. The enemies in this game aren't stupid; they don't stand around in one spot. A patrol might wander into your position, and cover gives you the edge.

CHEATING

"Cheat" and run the map borders to avoid enemies.

No, not cheat codes—the legitimate way to "cheat" on a mission is to hug the map's border. The mission boundaries are not endless, so you can skirt along one edge and gain the luxury of knowing an enemy cannot attack from that side. It's possible to travel deep into enemy territory this way and not meet a single hostile. The map border also provides a good retreat point. For those times when you're under heavy enemy fire, unsure of where the shots are coming from, beating it back to a border can give you a new launch point to redeploy.

NIGHT MISSIONS

Switch to night vision to see in the dark.

Nighttime is your best friend. While the enemy has its normal peepers that have trouble seeing very far in the dark, you can toggle on night vision and attack like an owl after a field mouse. Night missions allow you to move more quickly and usually give you the element of surprise. You can get a little closer than you normally would to assault an enemy location, thus increasing your accuracy and kill rate. Don't forget night vision on a day mission, either. Rather than stab around in the dark, flip on your infrared goggles inside a particularly gloomy building or underground parking garage.

ENGAGING THE ENEMY

Under fire, you want all your actions to be natural. Memorize the combat tactics in this section, and you'll be faster than the enemy.

It's the reason you've been called to this assignment—field combat. You've mastered the art of movement and learned the value of smart reconnaissance. Now it's time to engage the enemy. Under fire, you only have a split second to make the right call. Memorize these safety rules or carry along a body bag.

HIT THE DECK

If you can't find cover, your best defensive bonus comes from lying prone.

The single most important rule in combat is when you see the enemy, go prone. This makes you a harder target to hit and increases your accuracy since you can steady your weapon on the ground. From a prone position, search for enemies and line up your sights before they spot you. If you're in a vulnerable position—say, in the middle of an open field—crawl to the nearest piece of cover, then begin your enemy scan. For prolonged sniper reconnaissance, always stay prone to cut down on patrols spotting you.

MEMORIZE YOUR SQUAD

Do you need the sniper or demolitions? Make sure you know the order of your teams so you can toggle to the right guy quickly.

Before you take your first step, memorize the order of your teams. You can cycle through your soldiers using the map, starting with the first member of Alpha and ending with the third member of Bravo. Under pressure, you should skip to exactly the guy you need, so remember who you are at all times and how to get that support guy when you need the heavy artillery.

TIP

Don't be a hero. If an enemy has Alpha pinned down, take cover and bring Bravo in from a different angle to deal with the threat.

PINNED DOWN

The enemy is using real bullets. If you're unprepared, you die.

A bullet whizzes by your head—a second, a third. You can't figure out where the enemy is. After dropping prone, what do you do?

If the other men in your team aren't firing back, they can't see the hostile either. At this point, you don't want to get in a prolonged shootout. It will end up with you or someone else in the team biting it.

Take the best cover possible and switch teams. If Alpha is pinned down, toggle to a team member in Bravo and quickly identify the enemy's position. Most likely, the enemy is fully intent on putting holes in your Alpha team members. While he's occupied, move in quickly and unload with all of Bravo's weaponry. Once your threat indicator goes blue, switch back to an Alpha member and carry on.

COMMAND MAP

Avoid the body bag and peek around corners.

Think of the command map as your second team. You're in control of one team, and the computer controls the other from the commands you input on the map. Practice setting waypoints, adjusting arcs of fire, and reading the map symbols—and keep in mind the following tips.

TAKE CHARGE

Take charge of the primary fireteam on any given task.

The computer isn't a bad ally, but you're a bit smarter. Take charge of the key team whenever possible, whether it's finding good cover, engaging the enemy guard post, or running across open territory. Don't send an A.I. team into a nest full of enemies and expect it to clear it out. If you operate this way, you'll end up with too many casualties. The secondary team works great at covering your advance and defending a position.

CLEAR THE EXTRACTION ZONE

Clear out the extraction zone so you don't get sandwiched by enemies on your return trip.

Your first priority on a mission is to clear out the extraction zone if it's near the insertion zone. Obviously, you don't want to be moving into an ambush first thing off the chopper. More importantly, though, you want the zone enemy-free for the return trip. If you have to vamoose in a hurry, you don't want enemies chasing you into other enemies. Dying a few steps away from the finish line can be a little frustrating.

BONUS POINTS

If you let the enemy escape, he'll be back with reinforcements.

Carry out the bonus objective *before* you finish the primary and secondary objectives. Be careful though. You don't want to botch the main mission seeking out the least important objective.

ENDLESS POSSIBILITIES

Experiment with your two teams until you like what you see. Once you get good at lobbing grenades around, you might want to load up on a ton of them and barrage the enemy. Same goes for support soldiers and their heavy artillery. It's possible to go in, guns blazing, and obliterate the enemy.

But that's the hard way.

With practice, your Ghosts will be ready for any mission.

The approach to take with your squad is stealth. You don't want the big support dude unloading while your sniper's climbing into position. You also don't want a single grenade discharge to clue the surrounding enemy in on your position. With two teams equipped as previously suggested, you will have the best chance to minimize casualties to yourself and the hostages you're out to save.

GHOST RECON™

GR MISSION 1: IRON DRAGON

Your first mission isn't a cakewalk. The map is large, with enemies spread out all over the place. Your goal is to capture the rebel general, Bakur Papashvili, but first you have to live through his machine guns, snipers, and grenades.

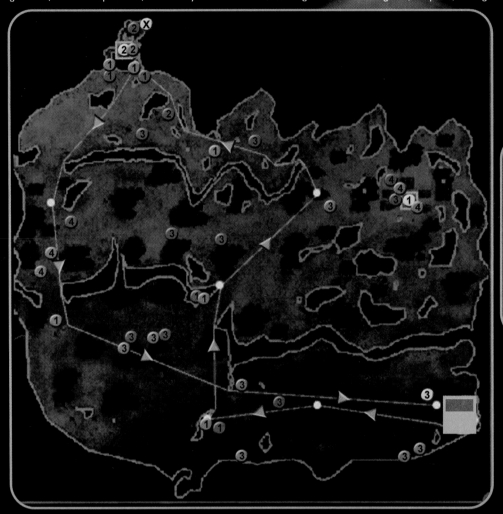

LEGEND

- ① Number of Enemies at Location (PS2)
- ① Number of Enemies at Location (GameCube)
- ① Objective Number
- ● Stop Points
- ■ Extraction Zone
- ■ Insertion Zone

MISSION CONDITIONS

Mission Name:	*GR M01 Iron Dragon*
Location:	*South Ossetian Autonomous Region*
Date:	*04/16/08*
Time:	*05:45*
Weather:	*Clear*
Item Requirements:	*None*
Hidden Soldier:	*Will Jacobs (Weapon 3, Stealth 2, Endurance 2, Leadership 3, armed with an OICW/GL)*

OBJECTIVES

1. *Neutralize Tent Camp Troops*
2. *Secure the Caves*
3. *Return to Insertion Zone*
X. *Capture Papashvili*

PARK PLACE

Before you start, get your two teams in order. You want to command a team with a sniper, because he's your eyes for recon. If you take a support soldier, make sure he's in the second team. Your team is the quick attack force; the second team hosts the larger firepower. Also, with every mission, cycle through your guys and familiarize yourself with the platoon order so you can reach any one of your operatives. As you do so, toggle to the weapon you want each to use in combat.

The first enemy patrol lies in the trees over the first hill.

Take your team over the first hill. There's a thicket of trees down the hill ahead of you. Your first enemy patrol lies inside that tree patch. Drop your sniper to the ground and use the telescopic sight to search them out. With some patience, you can find them before they find you.

Your sniper can take one out. If you're good enough, your sniper might take out two, or even all three. The three guards aren't armed with anything special, so your team of three will make quick work of them. It's the first encounter—they're taking it easy on you.

Don't expose yourself until after you take out the lone soldier in the bunker.

BUNKER HILL

Continue west until your sniper spots the bunker. Keep the foliage in front of you. If you make a mistake and wander into the open field in front of the bunker, you might be toast. There's a lone machine gunner patrolling the area. Use your sniper to get a bead on him. Take him out before he has a chance to throw lead into your flimsy bushes.

Try to draw out the enemy at the top of the hill near the bunker. If you don't, expect a heavy firefight in the woods.

So far, so good, but it's about to get ugly. To your right, up on the hill, is another enemy patrol. This one sports three guards, one carrying a machine gun. The catch? You're not just fighting one patrol. A second patrol farther west reinforces the moment you fire on the first patrol. You need to kill six enemies and deal with two machine guns.

CAUTION

The enemies around the bunker are not afraid to toss grenades on your unsuspecting head. Pick them off before they have time to get fancy.

After you deal with the threat in this area, move Alpha into the cover of the bunker and ready the next phase of your attack.

What's the best course of attack? Wait till you can spot their silhouettes at the top of the hill. If you have team Bravo placed to unload on the hill—but not too close—use your sniper to assassinate one enemy and draw the others into a fight. The bunker might look like a place of refuge and good cover, but Papashvili's guards are wise to that trick and lob grenades from the woods above. Fan out in the woods at the bottom of the hill. If you shoot at the guards, they will come down the hill looking for you.

The eastern mountain pass is easier than the west.

This is one of the toughest shootouts on the map, so rattle off some grenades from a rifleman's M203. Because it's early in the mission and not a major chore to restart, use Alpha and Bravo in different setups to take down the enemy.

SNIPER'S NEST

This is one of the most difficult shots in the game; you must eliminate the enemy sniper on a ledge before moving to the mountain pass.

You want the bunker. Cross the open field and come up on the bunker's left side. Crawl under the bunker and come out on the other side with your sniper. You are on a small hill looking across the open fields at a big cliff in the distance. Unfortunately, there's a sniper's nest, and the guy can see all the way down the valley to your little bunker here. He can kill your entire squad if you try to cross the mountain pass he's guarding.

It's time to test your aim. You can barely see the sniper, so wait and watch for movement above the sandbags. It's best to hit him with the first shot. If you do not, the enemy sniper has a tendency to hide and zing lead down on your troops. After he's dead, you're free to cross to the eastern mountain pass.

After the sniper's out of commission, the eastern mountain pass won't be any trouble—until you get to the top.

PASS WORD

Don't take the eastern mountain pass lightly. Patrolling the plateau above are two teams of three guards each. They move back and forth between the tent camp (objective #1) and the western mountain pass. You might get the drop on them, but each squad carries a grenade launcher, so be prepared for some shelling.

On top of the eastern pass, two enemy teams patrol the plateau. Unless you strike fast, it won't be an easy fight.

Creep over the pass's rise. If a patrol comes by, it will barrage you. Set your sights through the trees to your left; the patrols show up there, hidden behind bark and leaves. If you have a clear shot with a rifleman, arc a grenade into their midst and hope for maximum impact, though it's a tough shot through the trees. Follow with a crossfire between Alpha and Bravo, then prepare for the next group of three.

POP TENT

You travel northeast toward the tent camp (objective #1). Because you removed the threat of wandering patrols, you can get close to the small tent village. Crouch in slowly, and when your sniper can see the building that looks like an outhouse, or the markings on the tents, have your men drop to a crawl.

Inch in close to the tent encampment, and your sniper will do damage.

Four guards move around the surrounding areas of the tents. Three guards mill about the campgrounds, one armed with a machine gun and another with a grenade launcher. Draw a bead on the camp; your sniper can try to take out as many enemies as possible in the confusion. Line up your sight on the campfire or the chair next to it. If you can zero in on the machine gunner or grenade launcher, so much the better.

Fan your two teams apart and catch the enemy in a crossfire. If you can't find a good flanking position (cover is sparse on the eastern side of the encampment), assault in force—hunker down all six of your men in the woods near the camp and fire. A grenade from a M203 on the campfire or a rocket from the M136 detonating in enemy central will set off the fireworks.

ROCKY MOUNTAIN HIGH

After the tent camp, it's time for a cheat. Run along the northern map border, sticking to the mountain edge. The only enemy who can draw a bead on you must come from a southern or western direction. With this much protection, you won't have any trouble finding them before they find you.

 TIP

Use the map border to your advantage. Enemies can't attack you from the out-of-bounds areas.

Watch carefully along the emerging rocks. When an enemy appears, drop your team and scout the area. There are two guarding the upper reaches of the mountain range, though you only see one in front of a protruding rock. He's a "dumb" guard. He can't hear a shot, so come back to him later.

Don't shoot the "dumb" guard first; he doesn't respond to gunfire. Swing to your left and unload on the patrol in the open field.

From your current vantage point, you have a clear view of the plains in front of Papashvili's cave lair. Catch a patrol in the open. Waste the three guards —they have no cover behind which to hide. After you kill these three, swing back and take out the "dumb" guard. Wait 30 seconds, and his teammate comes out to play. Waste him, and you're ready to take on Papashvili's personal bodyguards.

THE CAVES

Objective #2 is in sight. There are two entrances to the cave system, a smaller crack to the west and the main entrance to the east. Don't go charging in—the enemy has the advantage of serious cover.

There are two entrances to Papashvili's caves. Launch a grenade into each to be sure no enemy remains.

Papashvili has one man guarding each entrance and two inside the caves watching both entrances. There are two approaches to storming the caves: stealth and brute force. The stealth approach involves patience—the shooting outside will draw one or both cave entrance guards to come out and take a peek. When they do, pick them off. The brute force method may work better here, however. If you have any grenades left, jettison one into the mouth of each cave. The blast kills most guards inside but doesn't reach deep enough to harm Papashvili.

TIP

Save some of your grenades in your riflemen's M203 (or extra frags) for the raid on Papashvili's caves.

Switch to night vision in the caves to gain the advantage on your opponent.

Even after your grenades, there might be one or two guards left inside the caves.

Don't go in the western entrance (the crack). It's harder to sneak through that way, and if any guards are left, they have a clear shot at you first. Choose the round eastern entrance. Switch to night vision to see in the darker corners, and send in a rifleman to find the remaining guard or two. Inch through the cave maze and peek to identify the enemies' positions. After you reach Papashvili's room, there are no more guards, and you have your prize.

Objective #2 is complete when you capture Papashvili.

THE TRIP HOME

Near the abandoned shack, look for the last machine gunner hiding in his bunker.

All that's left is to get to the extraction zone. Hugging the western side of the map, head down the mountain toward the western pass. There isn't much resistance left—enemies are lying in ambush near the extraction zone—but you can't freely advance. Depending on how fast you capture Papashvili, the remaining enemy team is somewhere along your route to your start position. You may encounter a machine gunner in the bunker near the abandoned shack or hiding in the woods. For style points, take him out with a rocket.

The last four enemies lie in wait near the extraction zone.

The last team of four is waiting in front of the extraction point, near your first encounter on the map. By this time, you should be a true veteran. Scope them out before they glimpse you, and clear the way to mission's end.

GR MISSION 2: EAGER SMOKE

Eight days after the successful raid in the South Ossetian mountains, it's time for another trip—this time a search and rescue on a secluded farm. Under cover of darkness, you must eliminate dozens of guards and free the pilot and weapons officer of a downed F18. You must also blow up the F18 before its technology falls into enemy hands.

Without night vision you couldn't see 10 yards in front of you on this mission.

LEGEND

- ⊙ **Number of Enemies at Location (PS2)**
- ⊙ **Number of Enemies at Location (GameCube)**
- ① **Objective Number**
- ● **Stop Points**
- ▇ **Extraction Zone**
- ▇ **Insertion Zone**

MISSION CONDITIONS

Mission Name: *GR M02 Eager Smoke*

Location: *South Ossetian Autonomous Region*

Date: *04/24/08*

Time: *02:15*

Weather: *Cloudy*

Item Requirements: *Demo charges*

Hidden Soldier: *Nigel Tunney, demolitions (Weapon 3, Stealth 3, Endurance 3, Leadership 3, armed with an SA-80 Carbine)*

OBJECTIVES

1. *Rescue Pilot*
2. *Rescue Weapons Officer*
3. *Get to Extraction Zone*
X. *Destroy Avionics*

D FENCE

Follow the fence along the eastern border to the barn.

The eastern map border follows a wire fence; stick to that path. Hug the fence to the southeast corner by the stream. You may not hit any resistance, allowing your teams to get deep into enemy territory undisturbed.

Time the barn guards' patrol route, and fire only when all three are in sight.

Watch for enemy patrols in the woods, along the stream.

You run into patrols in the woods to your right, about three-quarters of the way to the stream (where you first see trees by the fence). Use your sniper's scope and look for enemies along the ridgeline. They don't come as far east as your team, but they might take a potshot at you if they see movement in the dark. More than one patrol combs the woods at the top of the ridge, and they're usually in teams of three. Target them first then take them out.

HITTING THE BROADSIDE OF A BARN

Once you cross the stream, marine crawl up the hill until you see the barn. Don't stand, or even crouch, on the horizon; there are at least three guards who could spot you immediately. From your down position, inch forward until your sniper's sights are centered on the building. To your left, in the barnyard pen, one guard paces to the far post then back to the building. To the right, two guards should be talking near the entrance on the far side. Sometimes, those two guards disappear behind the barn, but they'll return. Occasionally, you can spot a single guard making his rounds inside the open barn doors.

Keep all three outdoor guards in sight at the same time. Once the shooting starts, maximize your impact. Begin with the guard on your left. Ideally, he's at the second part of his patrol and has his back to you as he returns to the barn. Shoot him first; he's the closest and poses the most danger. Immediately spin to the right and try to pick off both guards before they can retreat behind the barn or into the trees. If you can snipe the guard inside the barn, so much the better.

Shoot the enemy sniper in the second-story window, then swing over to the road to catch any patrols headed your way.

At this point, you have two worries. One interior guard moves to the barn's second-story window. Three enemies also patrol the road to your right and could come calling once shots are fired. Scan the road. If there are any troops there, open fire. More importantly, move in on the barn while the going's good. Send Bravo team straight to the wall of the barn (not the open barn door). Stay in control of Alpha and your sniper. Watch that barn window for the enemy sniper and prevent him from mowing down anyone from Bravo as they charge the barn.

Use the barn's back door to surprise the remaining hostage-takers.

Once Bravo is in position, leave it to guard the barn. If a patrol comes down the road later, Bravo should take care of it. Lead Alpha around the back. Head in the direction of the pen, and enter through one of the broken fence links. Keep a safe distance from the barn and, while moving, zoom in with your sniper's scope on the top window. Pick off the enemy in the top window just before you shoot the guy in the open door at the stairs.

⊕CAUTION

> If a seated hostage doesn't stand up, there are still enemies around. Don't try to rescue him until the area is cleared.

Freeing the pilot gives you objective #1.

If you've hit all your targets up to this point, there should only be one remaining guard inside the barn. Slide along the back door slowly until he comes into view on the left-hand side. Blast him as soon as a piece of him becomes visible. When the pilot stands up inside the barn, you have completed objective #1.

GIANT HAY ROLLS

You can expect at least one more patrol on the main road to the farmhouse.

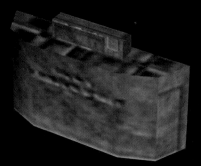

Depending on your luck, there could be a lot of dead enemies outside the barn at this point. If not, expect to encounter at least one patrol on your way to the next objective, the farmhouse. Scout the wooded areas west of the road carefully. Two patrols wander the trees, one with a machine gun. If you don't encounter them while taking on the barn, and if you hustle, you may not see them during the mission. There is also a group of three enemies on the road if you haven't killed them already.

Flank Alpha and Bravo about 30 yards apart, and angle toward the field on the east side of the house. Stay on the right side of the road to keep as far away as possible from the western enemy patrols. At the edge of the field, take Alpha toward the cover of the big hay rolls. Leave Bravo in the protection of bushes or in the trench that runs along the field.

TIP

There's a lot of enemy troop movement on this mission. If you restart a mission, don't count on the bad guys being in exactly the same position.

Recon the farmhouse carefully. There are at least two guards on the right side and one near the porch.

From the hay rolls, recon the farmhouse. No doubt at least one enemy guard is on his rounds. Pick off as many as you can with your sniper, then switch to a rifleman or Jacobs for his OICW. Pay particular attention to the porch at the south end of the house. One guard is definitely there, and you can sometimes snipe enemies at range through the porch opening.

Wander too far into the street behind the farmhouse, and the enemy will have you in his sights.

When you've wiped out resistance on the east end, slowly step on the porch and move to the western side. You pass a door on your right—it should be closed. If it's not, take care of the guards on the house's first level instead of moving any farther. Most likely, the door isn't open, so slug it out with the guards in the street on the house's west side. There are probably two guards left. Shoot them, or one will lob a grenade in your direction.

TIP

If one of your teammates yells, "Grenade!" forget what you're doing and immediately dive for cover.

One grenade wipes out the farmhouse's ground floor defense.

Now you're ready for the house. Open the door and quickly pump a grenade into the center of the room. Duck back behind the wall and wait for the explosion to take out the two guards on the first floor. Move upstairs until you can see the room across the open hallway. Don't step into the hallway and get shot. Peek to the right to see an enemy soldier hiding just inside the far room's doorway. Pick him off from what little you see; you can't get in the room without risking a bullet in the chest.

Upstairs in the farmhouse, shoot the hidden enemy in the room straight ahead, then round the corner and look for the last enemy next to the weapons officer.

Now move to the corner and peek into the hallway. You'll see the weapons officer in a chair and no one else. It's a ruse. There is a soldier guarding him, just inside the doorway. Inch down the hallway, sight extended, and shoot as soon as you see flesh. Once he falls, you've completed objective #2.

Rescue the weapons officer to finish objective #2.

TIP

Don't get the pilot or weapons officer shot. Assign them to the same team and have that team keep back from the action.

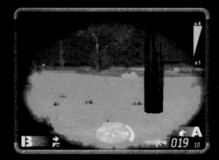

Watch out for a group of enemies behind the garage. They like to clip you in the back as you take off toward the F18.

DETONATE THE PLANE

Your last objective on your way back to the extraction zone is the downed F18. You don't have to plant the demo charge on the plane unless you want your hidden soldier unlocked for the future.

Hit the downed F18 on your trip back to the extraction zone.

Advance northwest, toward the F18 in the upper corner of the map. You might run into a squad of three enemies. They're on your eastern flank, so watch the bushes, trees, and hay rolls for movement. If that patrol opens up on you, don't advance too far or you'll get caught in a crossfire with the patrol milling about the F18. Always take care of one enemy group before moving to the next.

To complete the special objective, plant a demo charge on the downed plane.

As you've done before, use the hay rolls as barriers. Creep in as close as you dare to give your sniper a clean shot at multiple bad guys. You shouldn't have much difficulty if you take them by surprise. If there's no activity, send in your demo expert to drop the demo charge on the bird. Now get back to the starting zone.

HOMEWARD BOUND

Whatever patrols were in the southwest wooded area double back to stop you from returning to the extraction zone. Fortunately, the whole area is wooded and tough to navigate and get clear shots. Heading back, hug the northern rim of the map and head straight for the zone. Remember to hold your team with the two officers in the rear so they don't take fire.

Beware of stragglers waiting to ambush you.

At most, you should only encounter two or three enemies on the return, unless you veer too far south. Once the two rescued officers hit the extraction zone, the mission ends, and you can hang up your night vision goggles for the time being.

GHOST RECON™

PRIMA'S OFFICIAL STRATEGY GUIDE

GR MISSION 3: STONE BELL

Who said tanks were slow? On this mission, you have to be lightning quick to take out all enemy troops and prevent any NATO casualties. This may be the hardest mission in the game, considering you have about 10 minutes to complete the entire thing.

If you don't perform everything in record time, you won't survive this mission.

LEGEND

- ⦿ **Number of Enemies at Location (PS2)**
- ⦿ **Number of Enemies at Location (GameCube)**
- ❶ **Objective Number**
- ● **Stop Points**
- ○ **Allied Troops**
- ▪ **Insertion Zone**
- ⦿ **Tank**

MISSION CONDITIONS

Mission Name:	*GR M03 Stone Bell*
Location:	*South Ossetian Autonomous Region*
Date:	*05/02/08*
Time:	*10:00*
Weather:	*Clear*

OBJECTIVES

1. *Destroy Northeast Patrol*
2. *Destroy Southwest Patrol*
3. *Prevent HQ Breach*
X. *No NATO casualties*

Guard the Georgian command post with your life.

BREAKING THE RULES

You don't have the luxury of time in this mission. That means no hunkering down and waiting patiently for the enemy to show so your sniper can pop him. It's going to be a bloodbath, so consider yourself lucky if you complete the mission with only a soldier or two dead on your side.

 TIP

Sometimes it's necessary to split the two teams to complete objectives on opposite sides of the map.

Because there are two different patrols to take down on opposite sides of the map, you have to break the rule of working in tandem. Team Alpha must take out the northeast patrol while team Bravo eliminates the southwest patrol. They don't work together until the end of the mission.

There are three waves of enemies on the map. The first line of offense is the two patrols (objectives #1 and #2). You must take these out first and fast. The second wave is made up of three groups of soldiers, one following behind each patrol and one coming up the main road. Don't engage these troops, even if you have a clear shot, until *after* you take out both patrols. Why? The third layer of enemies is massive—two tanks, eighteen commandos, and lots of grenade launchers and machine guns. As soon as you engage a soldier in the second wave, the third wave begins to move in. To give yourself as much time as possible, you don't want that third wave moving until the last possible moment.

Team Alpha assaults the northeast patrol.

NORTHEAST PATROL

Take control of your sniper and run Alpha around the back of the HQ and up the mountain. At the top, slant northwest and head all the way to the edge of cover. Look between two rock outcroppings at the flats before the railroad track and the hill behind them. If you go at the start of the mission, you will intercept a team of three soldiers on the hill. Wipe them out before they have a chance to gain the cover of the rock to their right.

The second half of the northeast patrol comes from the railroad tracks to the east. Eliminate the first enemy, the one with the machine gun, before he can let loose.

Once all three are down, move forward and watch the tracks to your right. Keep your sniper's long-range scope on and advance. Eventually, the patrol's second squad emerges into view. Kill the first soldier to remove the threat of the machine gun, and mop up the other guy a few seconds later. Objective #1 is complete. Before you switch to team Bravo, move your Alpha soldiers to the railroad tracks in position to see the bridge.

Once the northeast patrol falls, run for the railroad bridge. Alpha should see the southwest patrol on its way to a meeting with Bravo. If you have time, help out by reducing the enemy number against Bravo.

TIP

The railroad bridge is the key to this mission. You must get your demo expert on top for a clear shot at the tanks.

SOUTHWEST PATROL

Though you don't control team Bravo until after Alpha takes out the northeast patrol, you do need to move it before this point. Just prior to taking control of Alpha, set Bravo's coordinates on the map. Click on the grove of trees just in front of the railroad car (see map at the beginning of this section). As Alpha charges up the hill to engage the northeast patrol, Bravo runs for position against the southwest patrol. From that vantage point, Bravo has the best chance to mow down the enemy without you in control.

From the trees near the railroad car, Bravo engages the enemy in force.

Once Alpha completes objective #1, take control of Bravo and shoot all enemies in sight. It's a tough gunfight. The reinforcements behind the first enemy squad of five come up quickly, signaling the tanks to begin their assault on the headquarters. That's why you left Alpha on the bridge.

Enemies love to use the railroad car as cover. As soon as you dispatch the first enemy wave, move up and use the car yourself.

Watch for enemies who sneak up behind the railroad car. They love to lie down flat and shoot you from underneath the cover of the big car. When the objective #2 complete box pops up—meaning you've killed all the soldiers in wave one—move up to the railroad car, and then flank the incoming enemy as best you can. Kill as many enemies as possible so you can help Alpha stop the main threat from overtaking the HQ. Expect a team of four enemies with a grenade launcher to come from the northwest.

TANKS A LOT

It gets really tricky here. You have three things to worry about: a team of four enemies advancing on the road, a team of four advancing up the eastern side of the map, and the tank division in the rear.

TIP

Let the NATO soldiers deal with stray enemies who wander down the main road.

Arm your rocket launcher and target the enemy tanks before they reach the bridge.

Forget about the first team of four on the road. You don't have time to deal with them. The NATO soldiers will take care of them with their machine gun. You have to move fast enough to prevent the patrol pushing ahead to the east from overtaking you before the tanks arrive.

Your main responsibility is the tanks. If they get too close to the HQ, the mission is over. Plus, the firepower on the tanks can obliterate you in seconds. Take control of your demolitions expert, probably Nigel Tunney, and ready the rocket launcher. Crouch over the northern edge of the railroad bridge, where you can get a clear shot at the road. Ignore enemy fire and zero in on the closest tank. Launch, and then repeat on the second tank. You must hit them on the north side of the bridge to keep your NATO friends from taking casualties. If you destroy the tanks on the southern side of the bridge, you will lose the special objective (and your chance at unlocking the hidden soldier). If you have an extra rocket left, launch it into the heart of the advancing enemy and hope for as much damage as possible.

It's possible to destroy a tank on the southern end of the bridge, but if you wait too long, the tank will overrun the Georgian command post.

By this point, the second eastern patrol is on top of you. Switch to your rifleman and hunt down the patrol quickly so you can join forces with Bravo and tag team on the remaining hostiles.

STRETCHED THIN

The enemy probably clears off the main road after the tanks are destroyed.

The enemy is crawling everywhere. You've successfully devastated their primary assault, but now the hostiles are scattered all over the place.

Identify where the biggest threat is hidden. This may take several reboots as you send Alpha and Bravo around the map waiting for the threat indicator to glow red. Try different directions until you know where the dozen or so bad guys are going to strike.

Locate the biggest enemy threat and converge both teams on it.

The highest priority now is keeping everyone at the HQ from getting shot. There are two officers inside the HQ; if they get shot, you immediately lose. Leave a fireteam nearby to guard against a sudden enemy run on the headquarters. Position a soldier on the cliffs on either side of the bridge so you have a clear shot at troops trying to make a frontal assault down the road. From the cliffs, you can also get down to the building quickly enough to prevent serious harm.

If you fear a sudden ground assault on the HQ, position one soldier on the cliffs to oversee all avenues of approach.

If you're confident that the majority of the remaining enemy is on one side of the map, or if they're still far away from the HQ, then bring your teams together and go hunting with the standard practices of flanking and crossfires. This cleans up the enemy more quickly, with less chance of injuring your men.

More than likely, though, you need to keep your teams split to guard the eastern and western hills from enemy incursion. Let the NATO soldiers take care of the road—unless the strongest force advances straight ahead—and pick off any enemy teams that threaten on either side. Plant your guys in strong cover, and they shouldn't have a problem dealing with incoming enemies, even if you aren't in control of the team.

After the tanks are destroyed, the enemy usually tries to make a push up the western flank. Reinforce team Bravo if you can.

WHEW!

Congratulate yourself if the HQ is still standing and none of your soldiers have a scratch on their helmets. This mission tests your ability to react under pressure and your speed in working two independent teams. Handle this one and you have definitely advanced well beyond beginner.

There's a lot of carnage on the road when you get through with this mission.

GR MISSION 4: BLACK NEEDLE

Your missions aren't always about killing people; sometimes they're about saving people. This time the Russians have pinned down a group of U.N. troops, and it's your job to open up an escape route for them.

Don't panic if you hear firing at the start of the mission. No one's shooting at you—it's the firefight in the village between the U.N. peace-keepers and the Russians.

LEGEND

①	**Number of Enemies at Location (PS2)**
①	**Number of Enemies at Location (GameCube)**
①	**Objective Number**
●	**Stop Points**
○	**Allied Troops**
■	**Extraction Zone**
■	**Insertion Zone**

MISSION CONDITIONS

Mission Name: *GR M04 Black Needle*

Location: *Republic of Georgia*

Date: *05/07/08*

Time: *15:00*

Weather: *Clear*

Item Requirements: *None*

Hidden Soldier: *Susan Grey, rifleman (Weapon 3, Stealth 2, Endurance 3, Leadership 6, armed with an M16/M203)*

OBJECTIVES

1. *Secure the Crossroads*

2. *Contact the U.N. Troops*

3. *Return to Extraction Zone*

X. *Keep U.N. Soldiers Alive*

Which one do you shoot first, the guard at his post or the patrol?

BRIDGE ON THE RIVER DIE

Directly in front of you and over the hill, southwest from the insertion zone, a road winds past a guard post and over a steel bridge draped in fog at the far end. Seems innocent enough—until you notice the rebels with automatic weapons patrolling the area. There's a single guard in his shack and a soldier along the trees to the southeast.

CAUTION

If you let the guard posted at the bridge escape, he'll alert everyone at the crossroads. Not a good thing.

Go for the group of three first. Your rifleman needs to at least pick off the one with a grenade launcher to minimize the threat to your team. However, you can't let the guard at the post escape. If he hears firing, he'll run across the bridge and alert his comrades on the other side, who will then be set up a defensive perimeter. Kill the wandering patrol quickly, then swing over and clip the guard post soldier before he gets too far across the bridge.

Before you go down the road, snipe the guard at the bridge's far post.

Once those four fall, advance down to the bridge. Zoom in on the guard post on the far side and shoot that guard before he gets active. Bring Bravo down and set its members in the trees on the eastern edge of the bridge—they can help with cover fire as you assault the crossing.

No matter what you do, you eventually bring the entire enemy force guarding the crossroads (objective #1) to the bridge. When the shooting starts, have everyone join in. In total, there are nine enemies to take down, two with a grenade launcher and one with a machine gun.

The steel bridge girders provide excellent cover. Weave in and out of them as you take on all the enemies at the crossroads.

Nearly all the enemy soldiers are grouped on the southern side of the bridge, so cross to the left side of the bridge with one of your heavy weaponry guys (like Jacobs with his OICW). Use the bridge framework as cover. Don't be thrown off by the metallic clunks as the enemy fire pelts the bridge—you have really good cover there. Lean over the bridge's side and pick off any troops in the woods south of the crossroads; there are usually three or four soldiers trying to hit you from the trees. Once those are eliminated, lean out roadside and pick off any enemies foolish enough to charge up the street. A few grenades from the OICW can make the work go quicker.

THE CROSSROADS

Beware the sharp-shooter in the shed, as well as the two around back.

The second western woods patrol can be quick. Be careful it doesn't get the drop on you.

The crossroads is empty now, so cross to the northwest and move toward the shed with the open door. From its cover, you have a clear shot down into the open expanse in the woods. Two patrols of three men each search the woods. Sometimes one of those patrols hangs around the shed, so be careful. Wait till you catch one of the patrols out in the open, then unload. You'll have to go looking for the second patrol, as it's now alerted to your presence.

Don't wander too far northeast toward the village. At the beginning of the mission, the U.N. troops in the firefight with the Russians are given "invulnerability" status so they don't die too quickly. Twenty seconds after you pass a special trigger zone—about halfway between the crossroads and the village—the U.N. soldiers lose their invulnerability. After that, they're fair game and won't take long to fall to the overwhelming Russian force. You're on a clock, and you'd better not falter on the way.

Eliminate the first patrol in the western woods before moving up to the village.

 TIP

Once you engage the village, the U.N. peacekeepers have 20 seconds of "invulnerability" left. Attack quickly, or they'll get shot down in the streets.

RAPID-FIRE RESCUE

Split Alpha and Bravo for another two-pronged attack. Taking Alpha through the woods to the west and Bravo up along the eastern section of the road.

Team Alpha has a choice: Sneak up close on the enemies firing at the U.N. peacekeepers, or simply let loose on their backs.

Alpha goes first. There are four enemies positioned outside the village walls, just on the other side of the big rock you circle around to the north. You should get the drop on these guys; their attention is on the U.N. peacekeepers inside the village. You can try to sneak up on them, and you might even take them all out without causing any suspicion. However, you're on a time clock, so you might prefer brute force measures here—sight all your team on four backs and open fire.

TIP

Tag team Alpha and Bravo to take out guards on either side of the village so they can't converge on the undermanned U.N. forces.

Team Bravo creeps up along the main road and picks off the machine gunner in the village.

When Alpha succeeds with the four outside guards, switch to Bravo. Position it to the east of the road, just before the horizon reveals the village. A few steps more brings you into direct firing range of two Russians, one wielding a mounted machine gun. Quickly spring over the horizon and shoot the two guards before they can return fire.

You have to battle enemies within the cover of broken ruins.

There are four Russians left inside the village ruins. Search them out before they can harm the U.N. peacekeepers. Move Bravo to the corner of the nearest village wall and move back and forth between walls until you've identified and killed all hostiles. Find the U.N. soldiers and you've accomplished objective #2. Now all you have to do is get out alive.

Meet up with the two U.N. peacekeepers to complete objective #2.

MASSIVE REINFORCEMENTS

As soon as you "rescue" the U.N. peacekeepers, reinforcements arrive on the road at the southwest corner of the map. A quarter of the force on the map—10 enemies—shows up with these reinforcements. Two enemy teams deploy and entrench to harass you on the return trip.

The southwest road at the crossroads spawns new enemies when you rescue the peacekeepers.

CAUTION

The road trailing off to the southwest seems harmless when you pass by it the first time. Once you rescue the U.N. soldiers, though, 10 enemies appear there as reinforcements.

Don't be concerned if the peacekeepers don't come with you. One probably will; the other likes to stand guard in the village. As long as you return to the extraction zone, and neither of them dies during that time, you complete the mission with the bonus objective.

Half the reinforcements guard the crossroads on your return trip.

Move your teams back down the main road. Hug the eastern flank again for maximum cover. When you come to the rise, duck down and scout with your sniper. Half of the enemy is set up at the crossroads. Sometimes they camp in buildings and in the western woods, but most likely they're right in front of you in the patch of cover where the road banks to the southeast.

Be prepared for a vicious fight. Bullets hail all around you from bushes and trees. These enemies do a good job of staying hidden, so watch for the streaks of fire. Many times your sniper can pinpoint a guy through the foliage from the weapon discharge.

The second half of the reinforcements greets you at the hill by the first bridge post.

Proceed cautiously to the road and shoot anything that moves in front of you. Slide along the bridge's northern perimeter and scope out the hill from where you originally launched your attack. The rest of the enemies are hidden there. Most take up positions in the bushes on the hill. A favorite spot to fire from is the wall halfway up the hill. If you have any remaining heavy artillery—grenades and rockets—now's a good time to get rid of them. You only have a handful of enemies left. When your threat indicator goes blue, you can approach the hill.

When you think the mission's over, it's not. There are still one or two enemies hidden in the bushes at the extraction zone.

Don't be nonchalant—it's not over yet. There are still one or two soldiers on the far side of the hill. They hope to catch you with your guard down. Bring both Alpha and Bravo to the top of the hill, then either crawl to the other side searching for targets, or advance in force and outdraw the last threats.

GR MISSION 5: GOLD MOUNTAIN

Buildings replace trees and cars sub for bushes—the enemy remains the same, but the scenery's all different in your first urban assault mission. On this mission, you secure a bank, try to slink through city streets without getting spotted by snipers, and recon a downed helicopter. Consider yourself lucky if you don't run into the tank.

LEGEND

- ◔ **Number of Enemies at Location (PS2)**
- ◑ **Number of Enemies at Location (GameCube)**
- ➊ **Objective Number**
- ● **Stop Points**
- ■ **Extraction Zone**
- ■ **Insertion Zone**

MISSION CONDITIONS

Mission Name:	*GR M05 Gold Mountain*
Location:	*Tbilisi, Republic of Georgia*
Date:	*05/14/08*
Time:	*09:00*
Weather:	*Clear*
Item Requirements:	*None*
Hidden Soldier:	*Scott Ibrahim, rifleman (Weapon 3, Stealth 5, Endurance 4, Leadership 3, armed with an MP5-SD)*

OBJECTIVES

1. *Secure the Bank*
2. *Investigate Crash Site*
3. *Go to Extraction Zone*
X. *Avoid Civilian Casualties*

URBAN COMBAT

Enemies have the element of surprise in urban combat. They are entrenched in buildings, like the bank you'll be clearing out. Enemy snipers can pop out of windows and gun you down before you know it. On the wilderness maps, there are a lot of open expanses you can take advantage of by catching the enemy exposed. Not so here, where the enemy can quickly duck behind cars or run down alleys.

As always, stay sharp. Take advantage of urban obstacles as cover—cars, garbage cans, fences, building corners, etc.—and stay out of sight in alleyways and building alcoves whenever possible.

> ### ⦿TIP
> There are five civilians who run across your path during the mission. To complete the bonus objective, control yourself and your itchy trigger finger.

At the corner of the starting area, wait for the two enemies in the first patrol to show, and then mow them down with automatic weapons. If you miss one, he'll try to sneak up on you from the protection of the nearby cars.

BANK HEIST

The first enemy patrol does a figure eight route around the bank and the building directly in front of the extraction zone. The patrol consists of five enemies, one with a machine gun. Identify the machine gunner because he's the most dangerous threat. Take him out first. Wait by the corner of the starting point and lie flat. Switch to someone like Jacobs with his OICW and click on full auto. The lead guard is about 10 feet in front of the others, and he pauses before continuing his march—don't blast at him, or you'll warn the others. Once you see all five guards in full view, sweep across them with automatic fire and drop them before they can reach the cover of the nearby cars.

Hold your fire on civilians.

The bank is much, much tougher to clear out. Steer to the left of the first building, and approach the bank from the side farthest from the main doors. You don't want any thugs inside the bank to spot you. Head to the street corner and have your sniper fix on the second story. There are two machine gun snipers poised to make life very unpleasant. Stepping right, zoom in on the first window, and as soon as you see the assassin's shoulder, pick him off. Do the same to the other sniper *after* you take care of the bank lobby.

The bank window snipers have a great view of the street. Zero in on them before they see your squad.

Grenades from your rifleman's M203 should reduce the bank lobby to quiet rubble.

TIP

Grenades should be used to clear out a room full of enemies. Toss one in and stand back.

Going in the bank's front door is asking for trouble.

Should you need to go to the second story, take the left door that leads upstairs and peek around corners until you identify where the bullets are coming from. With the railing at eye level, your best shot is to drop prone and shoot below the belt. You've probably taken the machine gun snipers out by now. If not, you can access their rooms on this level and surprise them from behind. Give your threat indicator one last check and remove any last hostiles on your way to claiming objective #1.

Going in the front doors is like sticking your hand in a hornet's nest. Cycle to one of your men with a grenade launcher and zip one in the front doors. You get casualties, but not everyone. Angle down till you can see straight in the bank and launch a second grenade. With any luck, you can take out everyone. Be careful, though—there is a guard on the second-story balcony, and sometimes two guards in the back room are protected from the blasts.

One or two guards might be hiding on the balcony and survive your grenade explosions.

ALLEY SHORTCUTS

Head out the back door of the bank to an alley directly north of you. Run everyone across the street and into the alley, avoiding five enemies who patrol the underground parking lot below the building to the east.

Avoid the enemy patrol in the neighboring underground parking lot by taking the alley at the bank's rear exit.

TIP

Why fight everyone? Navigate the streets properly and you can avoid more than a dozen soldiers on this mission.

Take the alley north, and at the T-intersection, head left (northwest) toward the helicopter crash site. Cross the open street and look for the next alley north of you. Watch carefully—on the east end of the street where it forms a four-way intersection, a five-man patrol circles back and forth between the extraction zone on the embassy building and the hotel to the north.

On the street between the bank and the downed helicopter, be on the alert for a patrol at the northeast intersection. You can avoid it by taking the first northwest alley.

Head north up this alley, but stop and go prone when you hit the wooden divider just short of the street exit. You're going to run into a patrol here. It's easier to fight in these cramped quarters, where the enemies can't draw a sight on you and you can see into the street. Be patient. Set your sight in the center of the opening. As soon as you shoot one, the rest come (you may have to deal with reinforcements from the five guards in the hotel to the northeast). Given time, it'll become a bloodbath, clearing the way for a free path to the downed helicopter.

Before the helicopter park, wait in the alley and set your sights on the main street for enemy activity.

The park lies at the northernmost reaches of the map. You have to get pretty close to examine the pilot. Unfortunately, the pilot's dead, but you still complete objective #2. Double time out of there; it's a very vulnerable area with very little cover.

Here's the downed helicopter and its fallen pilot.

⊕ CAUTION

The downed helicopter isn't a pretty sight. And if the enemy catches you in the exposed park, you won't be a pretty sight either.

THE EMBASSY BATTLE

Retreat to the first alley. At the T-intersection, hang a right this time. At the alley's end, drop prone and peek around the corner. There are at least two soldiers in the street. Snipe one, then the other.

Enemies pour out of the embassy at you. Watch the fire escape high and the street low.

Now drop back a bit and rise to a crouch. Center your sights on the fire escape and the courtyard archway on the south end of the embassy. Your two shots have alerted the guards. Alternate between the fire escape and the archway and shoot anyone who emerges to keep the enemy from reaching you.

Three snipers hamper your progress to the embassy rooftop.

Four guards patrol the embassy grounds; three snipers sit on the rooftop. Don't let an enemy rush at you out of the archway; but your main concern is the snipers since they have better accuracy. Hit the sniper on the middle roof first. Then focus on the right side, where two soldiers should come down the fire escape to get a better shot at you. Once the body count reaches seven, advance on the embassy.

⊕ TIP

Focus on the three snipers on the embassy roof. They have the greatest accuracy and pose the gravest danger.

Your final threat comes from the guards on the embassy grounds.

One important note: On your way to the helicopter, you may have evaded the five-man patrol at the embassy's northwest intersection (the one with the ruined building). If so, expect five more guns to reinforce the area. They do everything in their power to stop you from reaching the extraction point on the roof of the embassy. Proceed carefully.

When you think the embassy grounds are clear (and they probably aren't), keep your point person keyed on the embassy/courtyard archway and move Bravo across to the embassy's corner. Then move Alpha with Bravo covering. Get one of your men on the roof if you still have shooting to do.

GR MISSION 6: WITCH FIRE

Thousands will die if you fail your mission. Under the cover of darkness, you must infiltrate a medieval fortress and recover the Russian battle plans for their attack on the Latvian border. The war could get worse if your team doesn't return successfully.

LEGEND

- ① *Number of Enemies at Location (PS2)*
- ① *Number of Enemies at Location (GameCube)*
- ① Objective Number
- ● Stop Points
- ▤ Extraction Zone
- ■ Insertion Zone

MISSION CONDITIONS

Mission Name:	*GR M06 Witch Fire*
Location:	*Izborsk, Russia*
Date:	*06/06/08*
Time:	*02:00*
Weather:	*Clear*
Item Requirements:	*Antitank rockets*
Hidden Soldier:	*Buzz Gordon, demolitions (Weapon 5, Stealth 3, Endurance 5, Leadership 3, armed with an MP5)*

OBJECTIVES

1. *Gather Intel from SE House*
2. *Gather Intel from NW House*
3. *Get to Extraction Zone*
X. *Destroy SAM Site*

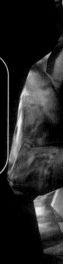

NIGHT MOVES

The southeast intelligence house, your first objective, looks innocent from a distance.

From the starting point, head east to the open field. Four soldiers live in the house north of the field. Eliminate them first, or you'll get caught in a crossfire later. If you stray too far north toward the house, guards around the fortress will spot you. Take them out at range.

Watch the road at all times. Troop transports travel this road, and you don't want to add their firepower to the confrontation. Cross Alpha over the road and into the woods to the east. Leave Bravo prone and facing the road's south end. A troop transport will be along soon; ambush it.

Place Bravo along the road to ambush the troop transport.

Head Alpha north through the cover of the woods toward objective #1, the southeast house. When Alpha fires on the guards around the southeast house, the game triggers a three-man truck on the road's south end. Bravo is in position to ambush this truck and prevent the reinforcements from arriving. Don't jump over to Bravo; concentrate on Alpha and its siege of the house.

HOUSE HUNTING

Get Alpha as close as possible. Take your prone sniper and inch in until you can clearly see the guards' faces. Four soldiers safeguard the Russian intelligence pictures. Two are talking outside the front door, while two others kick back inside. When you fire on the outside guards, the inside guards are alerted. Make quick work of the outside guards, then move to the house's front door.

When your sniper shoots on the first house, prepare for enemy return fire.

HOUSE TACTICS

• Circle the building and eliminate any outside guards.

• Look for clear shots through windows.

• Before opening the door, switch to your quickest weapon, like an M9SD.

• Open the door from a crouched or prone position.

• Peek around every corner and expect resistance until you've checked every room.

Open the door from a crouched or prone position and shoot anyone standing inside. The enemy tries to blast whoever opens that door, so be quick. Peek around corners until the room is clear. When the first objective window pops up, the coast is clear.

The Russian recon photos are your first objective.

MEDIEVAL TIMES

Can high-tech weapons beat a medieval castle?

Take a deep breath and prepare for a huge firefight. When the dust clears and the bullets stop whizzing, there are close to 20 dead Russians.

First, send team Bravo to the southwest fortress gate. Keep everyone low and out of sight; you don't want them to raise the alarm. They'll be ready for backup later.

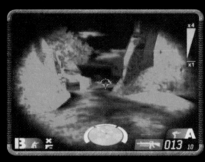

Team Bravo monitors the southwest fortress entrance.

Run Alpha to the southeast fortress gate. Most of the combat occurs from the gate's protective tunnel. Only move partially into the gate tunnel. It provides great defense from flanking enemy fire and the occasional grenade.

 TIP

When you lay siege to the fortress, fight from within the gate tunnels. They provide great cover from flanking enemy fire and grenade explosions.

Survey the fortress courtyard with your sniper. You should see two enemy groups of three: one group in the fields to the north, and another by the car in front of the second house. Each of these groups fights fiercely, but two enemies are designated as "runners." The runners duck and run for the ruins in the courtyard's northeast corner. If either makes it inside the ruins, he will radio for help at the communication station inside. A second troop transport will then enter from the north end of the main road and reinforce the battle with three more guards.

Six hostiles patrol the fortress courtyard. They aren't shy and shoot in your direction at first opportunity.

Snipe the six as soon as you can. If one or two entrench themselves by the houses or behind the car, have one of your riflemen arc a grenade on the spot. When all six soldiers are dead, move into the courtyard proper.

Two of the courtyard patrols run for the communication station. If you don't take them out, they'll radio for another transport with extra defenders.

Head northwest until you are almost in front of the main entrance (due north). Control your sniper, and zoom in on the house outside the main entrance to the north. Five soldiers patrol out there. You can bypass them now, but if they hear gunfire, they'll reinforce at an inconvenient time and drill your back. It's better to engage them now before other enemies join in. Your sniper has a clean shot at them all, while they'll have a difficult time shooting into the courtyard.

The patrol outside the northern entrance will show up if they hear gunfire.

Your next target is objective #2, the northwest house. When you shoot at anyone in the northwest house, guards pour out of the other two houses. You have to deal with 12 enemies in total, some with machine guns and grenade launchers.

Swing around to the north face of the house. You should see two lit windows with clear shots into the house. Shoot the first enemy you see, then shoot a second enemy when the first one falls. Proceed to the second window and see if you can take another shot.

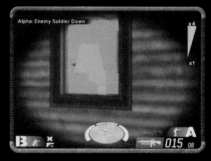

At the northwest intelligence house, snipe through the windows and pick off the unaware.

Prepare for the enemy storm. Go prone and switch to the soldier closest to a corner. You must do a lot of firing in the next two minutes, and you want control of the soldier with the best view.

TIP
While Alpha has the enemies occupied, Bravo can sneak in the fortress's southwest gate and take them by surprise.

Click on the map to pause the game and coordinate Bravo's sneak attack. Zoom in on the courtyard and select a spot at the southeast corner of the second building. This brings Bravo behind the main enemy threat and gives the team full access to the rest of the courtyard. Bravo causes enough havoc to split your enemies' attention, and your crossfire should mop them up within a few rounds.

The Russian top-secret maps are objective #2.

When your threat indicator turns blue, enter the northwest house. Don't take anything for granted, and make sure the house is clear before grabbing the top-secret maps and completing objective #2.

SAM I AM

Your last trip is the special objective, the mobile SAM site. Since you have a few rockets left, why not blast the enemy missile launcher? Head west out the fortress's southwest gate, and at the top of the hill you should see it.

Catch the enemy guards near the SAM when you hit it with the trusty rocket launcher.

A patrol of three guards surrounds the SAM. After the workload you just finished, this is a walk in the park. Switch to your demolitions expert and arm the M136. Wait until all three guards, or at least two out of three, are near the SAM. Stand up and launch the antitank rocket directly at the SAM's center. One shot should finish off the special objective, and if the blast radius is large enough, it'll take out the guards. Whatever enemies are left after the blast will be disoriented. Either pick them off from the hill, or if you don't have a clean shot, circle some of your men around the south and charge in for the kill.

 TIP

The rocket launcher can obliterate four or five enemies in a single explosion. When you have time, watch an enemy patrol route and try to catch them bunched together for maximum casualties.

TO THE RAFT

Look out for straggler patrols who might stop you from reaching the extraction zone.

All that remains is to return to the extraction zone. Remember the team of five guards around the northern house. They must be dealt with if you haven't done so already. Also, if a runner managed to reach the radio station, reinforcement soldiers could be milling about. If the mission hasn't ended when you take out the SAM, then you have some more to worry about on your return trip. Head north toward the upper reaches of the map, then go northeast. Scour the woods on the way and catch sight of the enemies first, then move in or avoid them if they're far away. With luck, you won't have any challenges on your way to the escape raft.

The military can't afford a helicopter this time. A raft is your means of escape.

GR MISSION 7: PAPER ANGEL

Every good commando team eventually blows up a bridge. Your team is no exception—the bridge over the Lubana River must be destroyed to halt the Russian armored advance. Bring the bridge down and you gain valuable time for the American forces.

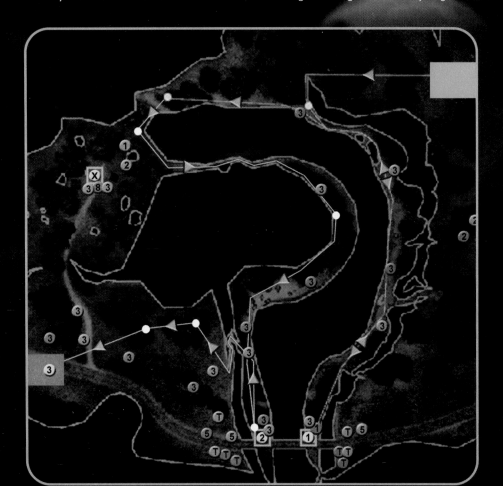

LEGEND

- ① *Number of Enemies at Location (PS2)*
- ① *Number of Enemies at Location (GameCube)*
- ❶ Objective Number
- ● Stop Points
- ▮ Extraction Zone
- ▮ Insertion Zone
- ⊤ Tank

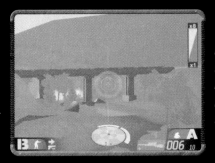

It may look pretty, but it's got to go. Bring the bridge down before the Russians can advance their armored division.

EAST VS. WEST

For the most part, water on this mission is just as hard as solid ground. You can't just go down to one bridge pylon and swim across to the other pylon to plant both charges. Only the shallow water in front of the Russian camp can be crossed— the rest is impassable terrain. The river makes this mission extremely long, since you have to go down the river's east side, then retrace your steps and wrap around to go down the west side. As convenient as the road bridge might be, you can't outshoot the troops that guard it, so take the long way around.

CAUTION

You can't swim the water in this mission. Under fire, seek cover behind the large rocks and dense bushes.

The first Russian patrol greets you around the first bend on the river's east coast.

Start by heading west from the insertion zone, and hook a left as the hill goes down to the river. There's a small access to the river's east side. Follow that small strip of land down to the first pylon.

Before that, though, deal with the Russian guards. Two patrol the northern half of the east coast. Wait for them at the first rock outcropping, then surprise them without a shot fired in your direction. As you advance south, use your sniper to survey the west coast. At any point, if you see enemies, drop prone and shoot. The more you take out now, the less you have to deal with when you engage that side.

As you advance down the east coast, scout the west coast for enemies. Any enemies you take down now speed up your travel time later.

Stick to the cliffs as you progress. Don't wander too close to the river. You present a good target to the soldiers on the far side. There are soldiers patrolling the cliffs behind you who would love to drop a grenade on your head.

TIP

The Russians have a nice range with their grenades. They can shoot them across the river, so make sure you're flush against the cliff wall when you annoy them.

The second east coast patrol walks the southern half.

On the second half of the coast, you run into two more enemies just south of the breach that winds up to the plateau. Snipe them from a distance, then turn your attention to the breach. You don't want enemies bursting your back open. Pass by the breach carefully, then call Bravo to come down and do the same.

Go slowly across the breach in the east coast cliffs. Guards can easily slip down behind you.

PYLON ONE

There's one guard defending the first pylon—and a couple of tanks. He can be silenced without a sweat; it's his friends on the bridge you should worry about. Don't try to take the bridge. Before you know it, you'll have a tank rotating its turret on you.

Don't fire at the bridge guards. Look for the single guard by the pylon and eliminate him.

After hearing a shot or spotting your movement below, a five-man squad descends the cliff stairs to the south of the pylon. Gun them down on the steps. If they make it to the bottom, you're toast. Once you have a 10-second block to rest, switch to your demo expert and plant a charge on the pylon. Objective #1 is complete.

When you near the first pylon, guards pour down the cliff stairs to engage you.

K.I.A. CAMP GROUNDS

Double-time it back to the insertion zone area. Head due west until you go downhill and near the river. The last shred of bushes is your destination. From there you can see the entire northern edge of the Russian tent camp (the mission's special objective).

Shake up the Russian river encampment with a few unannounced grenades.

Position a rifleman between the trees for an unobstructed view, and let loose a few grenades into the campground. Drop prone with the rest of your men, and wait for the hostiles to come to you. Eight angry Russians assault you if you miss with the grenades. No matter, though—with both your fireteams keyed on the shore, hardly any lead should blur by you. If you've done your job correctly, you won't need to leave the shore and get wet until it's time to take the river's west coast.

> ## TIP
> If you use a grenade launcher, don't lob the grenades too far into the Russian camp. Most of the enemy rings the northern end of the compound, and you'll miss if your frag hits the campfire itself.

A WALK ALONG THE BEACH

A concealed passage takes you to the river's west shore.

After vanquishing the Russian camp, head left and search for a concealed passage through the rocks. The passage winds down to the river's west shore. If you miss this and head south, you'll walk into a nest full of enemies. You'll fight them later, so steer clear to gain the element of surprise when you really face off against them.

Around the west shore's first large bend, a three-man patrol watches the beach. You should have already taken care of them from the east shore, but if not, don't let them get the drop on you.

It's clear sailing on the west coast if your sniper did his job on the east side.

At the end, three Russians guard the second pylon. It's tricky here—you must sneak up on the three pylon guards; however, the enemies on the bridge usually spot you and start shooting. If you can find a safe spot for your sniper to settle down for a long-range shot, go for it. More than likely, you need to switch to one of your riflemen, or even a demo guy with his M4, and rush the three, blasting away with semiautomatic speed. Take down the patrol and make sure all three of your team members are under the safety of the overhanging bridge. Setting a demo charge gives you objective #2.

> ## TIP
> In close gunfights, use automatic weaponry like the OICW or the MP5-SD.

Enemies descend from the plateau above when you try to destroy the second pylon.

Now you've got to get out. All this commotion brings more troops. A group of three enemies hangs out on the plateau near this side's breach to the top. They descend the breach and try to find defensive cover on the shore before you return. Shoot them on the shore; it's too difficult a shot from your current angle. Alternatively, you could set up Bravo near the big rocks halfway down the shore as backup to cover the ledge. Whether you decide to take them on yourself or not, your sniper or rifleman should drop them.

Veer to your right at the top of the west coast breach and head for the protection of the nearby trees.

When the way to the top is clear, run to the top and veer right toward the nearest trees. You want cover immediately so the tanks and remaining enemy on the bridge don't barrage you. Bring Bravo up, and together move to the top of the hill, but not too close to the rise.

SECLUDED FIREFIGHT

The extraction zone is in sight, but you can't reach it yet. Six enemies guard the road at the bottom of the hill, two armed with accurate grenade launchers. If you linger in one spot too long, you can expect a grenade to rain on your parade.

Six enemies secure the final road before the extraction zone. Catch them in a cross-fire between Alpha and Bravo.

Both teams should go prone and crawl into position. Take Alpha and slide to the south side of the woods. Bravo crawls to the north end of the woods. It will take a while to set up a good crossfire. One group of enemies hangs near the road intersection, so Alpha must take it out. Wait till it moves closer to the second enemy group, though; you don't want it running up the hill and flanking you. The second enemy group is on the road centered between your two teams.

TIP

When setting up a shot, don't just accept the first place you find. Rocks and bushes can hide you from the enemy, but they also can block your shot. Keep cover away from your front firing arc.

Alpha fires first, picking off the guard farthest to the left. Start on the end and work your way toward the middle. If you chase the remaining enemies toward Bravo, your crossfire rips them to shreds. Hopefully, Bravo has a support soldier because he can open fire on anything that moves. Keep firing and don't give anyone a chance to throw a frag. A few enemies might make it to the woods—that just makes it an easier kill for you.

GR MISSION 8: ZEBRA STRAW

The mission's bogged down with a storm and the enemies' bullets rain down on you in Venta. Survive the initial firefight with the locals, and then escort a friendly tank through the war-torn village streets. Try not to get shelled.

Your soldiers are in for the fight of their lives, and some will end up dead if you aren't organized.

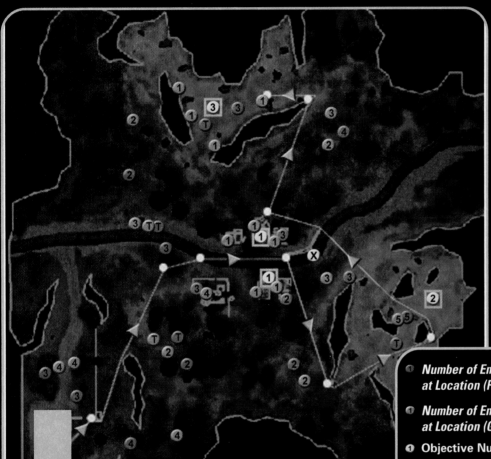

LEGEND

- ① **Number of Enemies at Location (PS2)**
- ① **Number of Enemies at Location (GameCube)**
- ● **Objective Number**
- ● **Stop Points**
- ■ **Insertion Zone**
- ⓣ **Tank**

MISSION CONDITIONS

Mission Name: *GR M08 Zebra Straw*

Location: *Venta, Lithuania*

Date: *06/24/08*

Time: *16:00*

Weather: *Rain*

Item Requirements: *M136s required*

Hidden Soldier: *Nigel Tunney, rifleman (Weapon 5, Stealth 3, Endurance 5, Leadership 5, armed with an OICW)*

OBJECTIVES

1. *Secure the Village*
2. *Destroy East Artillery*
3. *Destroy North Artillery*
X. *Protect Friendly Tank*

MASSACRE AT VENTA

Do everything exactly right or you're going to die. The mission drops you in the middle of a huge firefight. Eight enemies assault you as soon as you arrive—two teams of three from the north and one team of two from the east. The first few times you play the mission, you will lose people. Don't get discouraged—with a little practice, you'll get all your troops through unscathed.

The building ruins near the insertion zone are not the best place to take cover in the opening firefight.

Your closest cover—the building ruins immediately north of the insertion zone—seems like the perfect choice. It isn't. Though it's possible to kill the enemy from the building ruins, the fight will probably be a bloody one for you. From the "protection" of the ruins, it's hard to track all the enemies, and if they get close enough, expect a grenade in your midst.

Sending your rifleman to the shack/stone wall is the key to beating the early onset of enemies.

Send the first Alpha guy you control, probably a rifleman, directly toward the shack and stone wall just northeast of your starting position. Lodge yourself in the corner and crouch so your gun tip is slightly above the wall. You now have solid protection from bullets and grenade blasts. Plus, you can shoot the group of six enemies as they sneak over the hill in the distance. They come from your right, and you should be able to plug one or two of them near the tree on the hill. If they slip through, they will appear on the second hill to the left. That's the enemies' favorite place to throw a grenade. Shoot anyone on that hill first to avoid potential shrapnel.

Shoot the enemies to the north before they throw a grenade in your lap.

The two enemies to the east can't shoot you since the shack safeguards your back. Deal with the six on the hill first. Once all is quiet, you can swing around and help out your Alpha teammates.

The enemies to the east come over the crater.

Leave Bravo at its starting location. From there, the team can lend support against the enemies advancing from the north. Don't touch the other two men you have in Alpha; they should settle down to guard your back, which means watching the east and taking care of those two Russians. There should be a giant crater directly to the east; the two-man patrol peeks over that crater to fire at you. Shoot the enemies before they get a chance to reach for a grenade and you won't have a problem.

AIR STRIKES AND TREADS

Check for wounds after the starting shootout and send Bravo north to the road. A friendly tank soon spawns at the western end of the road and continues through the village to the eastern end of the map. You want Bravo to follow this tank, lending it cover fire, so toggle on the command map frequently to update Bravo's position.

Air support napalms one of the enemy tanks to help you out.

Alpha should head due northeast to the road. You need to get in front of the friendly tank and take out resistance, especially enemies equipped with antitank rockets. As you pass through the gap in the rock wall, air support bombards an enemy tank creeping in from the east.

Guard the allied tank to the end of the road, or you can't complete the mission's special objective.

When you hit the hill just before the road, control a rifleman with an M203 and target grenades on the enemy position to the north (you should see the enemy tank through the gray mist) and the east (a blown-apart church). Watch the church courtyard—there are three soldiers, and one of them has a rocket launcher aimed at your tank. A grenade in the general ballpark should wipe out the dangerous rocket. Just to be sure, zoom in with your M16 sight and blast anything that peeps out from behind the rubble. Unless it shoots at you, forget the enemy tank to the north. Your allied tank shreds it all by itself.

Your allied tank blows up the enemy tank to the north.

VILLAGE PEOPLE

The allied tank continues into the village. When the tank reaches the outskirts of the buildings, it is ambushed. You have to be there before it and handle the enemy.

Before the allied tank enters the village, you must destroy the enemy's antitank personnel.

You want Alpha and Bravo working together on this one. Run one team up the north side of the street and one team on the south. Unload one or two grenades on every single building in the village. Better to be safe than sorry. Your ever-faithful OICW works beautifully in these types of situations.

The first building on the left (north) hosts three enemies, one with a grenade launcher. These are the least important. Eliminate them to avoid hits, but if you have a choice of targets, go for either of the next two.

Enemies can come out of the gloom at any second. An itchy trigger finger is encouraged.

The second building on the right (south) conceals two heavily armed Russians. One sports a grenade launcher. The second, the bigger threat, wields a rocket launcher. If the allied tank enters the village, this Russian will fire his rocket, timed with a second rocket launch to the northeast. Shoot both enemies as soon as they expose themselves to aim at the tank.

The Russians near the village's second building have a rocket launcher.

The last building on the left shields three enemies; one has an antitank missile to use as soon as he sees the allied tank. You can't let these guys live long, so fire on them immediately.

If you're having trouble, save the game before the tank enters the village. Toggle back and forth between Alpha and Bravo quickly so you can get the best shot at the enemy. For example, Alpha on the south end of the road has a better shot at the first group of enemies, while Bravo on the north side can spot the second enemy group better. When the objective #1 box pops up, you can rest your trigger finger and stop worrying about the allied tank.

Get the tank through the village and it's home free.

EASTERN ARTILLERY

Even though the eastern artillery is the least defended, you still have to watch out for five soldiers.

The least defended area on the map is the eastern artillery battery. Five soldiers guard the area, but you can sneak in the back door. Head southeast to the most distant rock outcropping. Pick off guards as you move north through the rocks, but watch out for two in particular—one has a machine gun and another a grenade launcher. Stop at the eastern map border when you have a clear shot at the artillery. If you're positioned correctly, the artillery won't notice you, and you can shred it before any more allies go down in flames. Cross off objective #2.

The perfect ambush point for the eastern artillery lies in the rocks to its south.

WESTERN ARTILLERY

The western artillery battery can be tougher. Two patrols scour the flats in front of the artillery. The three-man squad to the west might have already been eliminated; they tend to wander south into the heavy shooting area once the allied tank strolls down the road. If you know for certain the three-man patrol is gone, head up the western mountain flank to gain access to the artillery battery.

Two patrols crisscross the flats in front of the western artillery while another guards the artillery's hill.

If not, face off against the four-man eastern patrol. There are plenty of craters to hide in across the flats, so use them as you move your teams in tandem. However, keep in mind that the enemy can do the same thing and suddenly pop up with a rifle barrel to your chest. Use your sniper to spot the enemy first. If you fail, the enemy with the grenade launcher will cork one in your direction and kill you.

The western artillery's wide open from its eastern flank.

After the patrol has been dealt with, head up the side of the mountain. Most of the enemy can be taken off guard. One enemy, however, likes to hide in a rocky crevice and rip your back wide open. When heading up the east side, watch the northern rocks carefully for movement. If you hear firing and don't know where it's coming from, set your sights north. As soon as you have an open shot at objective #3's artillery battery, launch away. It should detonate as smoothly as its eastern counterpart.

DRIPPING WET

No one likes to get wet. Worse, in the field, rain and fog make it difficult to pinpoint the enemy. Once you complete your eighth mission, you can rest assured that your team can operate under poor weather conditions and still come out a winner.

GR MISSION 9: BLUE STORM

Just when you thought the weather couldn't get worse, your superiors set you down in a bug-infested swamp. Swim between the dank reeds and shadowy marsh critters, and dodge enemy fire as you search for your objectives. While clearing three islands of enemy encampments, you must seize a Russian commanding officer from a house guarded better than Fort Knox.

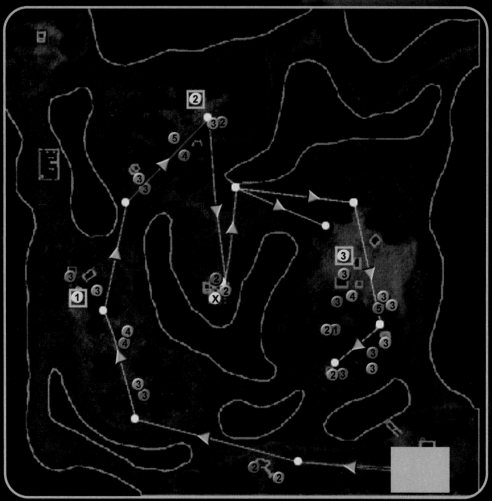

You get all the cushy assignments—a trip to Nereta Swamp.

LEGEND

- **①** *Number of Enemies at Location (PS2)*
- **①** *Number of Enemies at Location (GameCube)*
- **①** Objective Number
- **●** Stop Points
- **■** Insertion Zone

MISSION CONDITIONS

Mission Name:	*GR M09 Blue Storm*
Location:	*Nereta Swamp, Latvia*
Date:	*07/03/08*
Time:	*9:00*
Weather:	*Rain*
Item Requirements:	*None*
Hidden Soldier:	*Klaus Henkel, sniper (Weapon 5, Stealth 4, Endurance 4, Leadership 6, armed with an SVD)*

OBJECTIVES

1. *Clear Northern Island*
2. *Clear Eastern Island*
3. *Clear Western Island*
X. *Capture Russian Officer*

SWAMP MOVES

As far as range of vision goes, you're in the same boat as last mission—thick fog that dampens your senses. Enemies can ghost in and out of the fog. One second you're tracking a guard with your sniper; the next, he's gone. It provides cover for you, but there are a lot more bad guys running around.

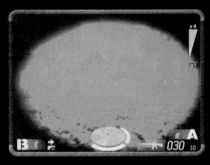

Is the enemy there or not? It's hard to tell in the fog, so watch for movement of any kind.

Establish strong defensive positions and only move when the coast is clear or semiclear. Unless the enemy is on top of you, Alpha and Bravo won't have difficulty setting up effective cross-fires. Switching to night vision outlines an enemy's heat signature against the background.

Swim the edges of impassable swamp water for maximum cover.

Take full advantage of the swamp water. Duck your men into its slimy cover and skirt the edges of impassable areas. Guards cannot patrol these areas, so even in the middle of the waterways, you have no risk of someone sneaking up on you. In the center of the map especially, you can move quickly and unseen past enemies.

ISLANDS OF ADVENTURE

Don't move north to the eastern island first. Twelve enemies—the biggest group on the map—dwell there, and you should only fight them when you have the element of surprise. The brunt of the enemy's eastern patrols range in the south of the island, and they have two bunkers set up—all to deter your starting force from going straight for the main encampment.

Travel west as long as you have land to stand on. It doesn't last long, and soon you see a fallen tree at the western edge of the starting landmass. Three enemies patrol this area. They're nonchalant, not expecting any activity, and will easily go down.

The first patrol is near the fallen tree on the way to the west island, objective #1.

Dive into the swamp and head northwest. In the distance is a flicker of white light. It's coming from a barrel fire on the western island. Head there and come up on the land west of it. Hunker Alpha and Bravo down on the crest of the hill and wait to ambush the first wandering patrol.

Set up an ambush west of the barrel fire for the next Russian patrol.

A four-man patrol comes through first. Its members love plopping a grenade on your position, so pick them off through the trees at long range. The longer the fight goes, the more trouble you're in. A second enemy patrol—this time three soldiers—can reinforce them from the northern stretch of the island. After the first patrol falls, flank out Alpha and Bravo on either coast and look to pin the second patrol between you as you walk north.

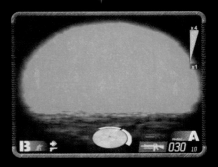

The first, four-man patrol on the west island can be backed up by a second, three-man patrol.

TIP

Should you lose the enemy in the fog, watch your threat indicator for a new direction to shoot.

PARADISE ISLAND

The north island is a paradise in the sunlight, but not right now. It's lousy with Russian assassins who wiggle in its mud and sleep in its trees.

To avoid a four-man patrol, you're going to head straight into a trap. North of the west island, four Russians march between the graveyard and the northern access route to the north island. You can ignore them if you head northeast through the marsh waters toward the north island. So what if there's a bunker with a machine gunner? You've beaten worse.

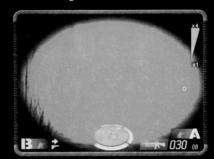

To complete the second objective, go through this machine gun bunker.

The machine gunner's asleep at the wheel. You can get close to him, chin deep in swamp water, and deliver a permanent message. Use a rifleman on semiauto or a support's M249; you want to spray bullets through the mist from here on out.

They look like you, but they aren't friendly. The assassins on the north island come out of nowhere.

The rest of the island's full of assassins. They're dressed like your sniper, complete with camouflage vines and long-range capabilities. Discounting the dead guy in the bunker, you have seven more enemies to handle. Grenades aren't effective against you in the water, so spread out your teams and shoot to kill. The enemy should come to you; it isn't long before you either receive the objective #2 completed box or you're sleeping with the fishes.

HAUNTED HOUSE

Against the stormy sky, the flooded house where the Russian commander stays looks intimidating.

At the map's center, the Russian commander's house sinks in the bog. Six bodyguards protect the house, half with machine guns and the other half with grenade launchers.

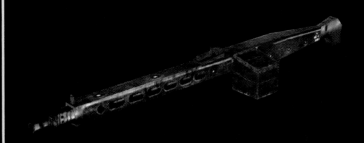

Look for bodyguards on the dry second floor or the flooded first floor of the commander's house.

Approaching the house from the northwest, head to the north side of the house and its ground-floor front door (the one on the porch). Switch to a soldier with the M249 on full auto. You need to be fast. Edge up to the door, then duck into the frame and spray the room with bullets before retreating. You don't get everyone because some are hidden behind posts. Repeat and move in against anyone still standing.

CAUTION

The game's most heavily armed enemy group guards the Russian commander. The six-man team carries three machine guns and three grenade launchers.

Usually there are five guards on the first floor and one upstairs. Watch for this guy; he runs down the stairs and shoots while your back is turned. Sometimes there are four downstairs and two upstairs.

Every once in a while, the commander is found outside his house. It certainly makes for an easy capture.

If you're not ready to fight, lay low in the bog and wait for the enemy to pass.

TREASURE ISLAND

From the commander's house, head due north. Don't angle in toward the eastern island, or you'll run into the enemy too soon. After you hit the impassable swamp region, work northeast through the swamp weeds to the island. There is no one home there, though the top of the hill holds the thick of the enemy encampment.

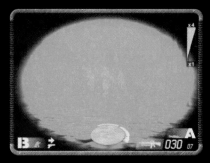

Park team Alpha at the top of the eastern island hill within sight distance of the enemy.

Send Alpha up the hill and drop prone near the top so you can inch in for a closer look. Place Bravo inside a nest of trees that also has a view of the encampment from the lower side.

Place team Bravo on the edge of the trees closest the encampment to catch anyone crossing the grounds.

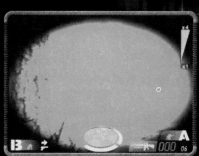

CAUTION

With all the commotion on the eastern island, don't shoot your companions by mistake.

Alpha has the best shot, so it fires first. Wait until at least three enemies are on the screen. When the enemies move to converge on Alpha, they cross in front of Bravo. Alpha needs to watch to the left—enemies sometimes sneak up that flank and shoot off a grenade. Three enemy teams of four soldiers each mill about the island, so you have a long battle on your hands.

Beware of the camou-flaged bunkers.

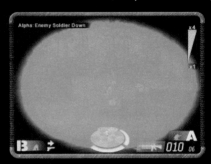

When the enemies try to converge on Alpha, Bravo knocks them dead.

After the shooting quiets down, you have to rally both fireteams to search the island for the stragglers. Beware of the camouflaged bunkers on the south end; the enemies inside can snipe you without you even realizing the bunker exists. After a bit of hide and seek, the enemy should fall, as well as objective #3, and your mission is complete.

You may have to hunt down the remaining bad buys to clear the final island.

GR MISSION 10: FEVER CLAW

Your eighth mission, when you guarded a tank through the village of Venta, was the minor leagues. Welcome to the majors, where you have to safeguard three tanks past a horde of rocket-toting lunatics and enemy tanks bent on lodging a shell in your cranium. Successfully guide the caravan to the city's cathedral, and you'll be rewarded with a well-earned day off.

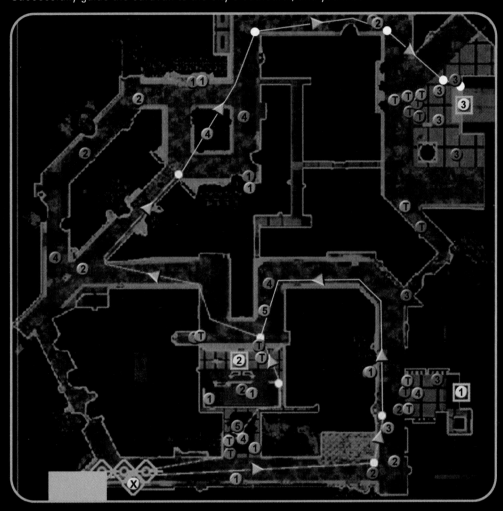

This mission is all about tanks.

LEGEND

- ① *Number of Enemies at Location (PS2)*
- ① *Number of Enemies at Location (GameCube)*
- ❶ Objective Number
- ● Stop Points
- ○ Allied Troops
- ◇ Allied Tank
- ■ Insertion Zone
- ⓣ Tank

MISSION CONDITIONS

Mission Name:	*GR M10 Fever Claw*
Location:	*Vilnius, Lithuania*
Date:	*09/01/08*
Time:	*18:00*
Weather:	*Rain*
Item Requirements:	*M136s recommended*
Hidden Soldier:	*Henry Ramirez, rifleman (Weapon 6, Stealth 4, Endurance 5, Leadership 5, armed with an MP5-SD)*

OBJECTIVES

1. *Secure University Square*
2. *Secure Presidential Palace Square*
3. *Secure Cathedral Square*
X. *No Friendly Tank Casualties*

SHELL GAMES

Don't mess around with an enemy tank. Without rockets, you can't harm the things, and each one can pick apart your entire team. The solution? Bring at least two demo experts on the mission, one per fireteam, and equip them with M136 Rocket Launchers. One dead-on shot from the M136 will kill the enemy tank.

The demo expert with his M136 becomes your team's MVP.

Tanks are not slow; they will outrace you through the streets of Vilnius if you aren't on top of things. Stay in front of the tank caravan the whole time to prevent enemies with rocket launchers from targeting the tanks. It's more dangerous for you, but that's why you're riding shotgun.

Fail to outrun the allied tanks, and the big bruisers will die against the enemy rocket launchers.

The enemy tanks are tough, and so are yours. The allied tanks can't handle a rocket to the turret; however, they can handle just about anything else. If there is no threat of an antitank missile, let your tanks do the cleanup work for you. Why risk your skin in a firefight with six enemies, when the tank mops them up in five seconds?

Duck for cover behind your tanks whenever possible.

You can also use your tanks as defense. Think of them as moving cover. Always position yourself on the opposite side of enemies without missiles, with the tank between you, and add support fire as you see fit.

If you can't destroy an enemy tank, don't sweat it. Hopefully, the overwhelming firepower of your three tanks will punch a hole in it. The mission doesn't end if you lose a tank—you just don't gain the special objective bonus—and you don't have to destroy any of the enemy tanks to complete the mission.

THE RUNNING MAN

Set your two teams up in the beginning while the tanks are idling because once you start running you won't stop. You *must* get ahead of the tanks to stop antitank missiles from destroying them. That's no easy task when the tanks are motoring at full speed.

Team Alpha runs at full tilt alongside the tanks.

Send team Alpha up the south end of the first street. Don't worry about Bravo for now—leave it at the insertion zone, safe from random explosions and shrapnel. Run Alpha full out to outdistance the tanks. Continue at a full run up the street. Only slow down when the lead tank rotates its gun turret to destroy the enemy tank in the Presidential Garden courtyard (halfway up the street on the north side). Your tanks can handle the match-up, so let them destroy the enemy tank and the three supporting enemies. Your job is to not get shot, then bolt when the enemy tank explodes. Even with this lead, the tanks catch up with you by the end of the street.

Wait for the enemy tank to explode to avoid its deadly gunfire.

TIP
Use the three allied tanks to attack the eight enemy guards in the university courtyard.

At the east end of the street, before you turn the corner toward University Square, two enemies take potshots at you. Shoot the guy on the left. He shows up first, and you need to have control of that street corner to set up your attack on the university. Most of the time you can ignore the guy on the right; the allied tanks are on your heels and gun him down as an afterthought.

The man on the corner isn't selling magazines; he's got his sights on you.

END OF THE WORLD U.

The toughest fight comes from the book learners. The enemies defending the university will destroy you if you aren't careful. Don't let all their firepower distract you. As you turn the corner, your eyes should be set on one person.

Wait for your tanks to arrive and support you at the university. Don't let the rocket launcher destroy them.

When the tanks enter the university area, one enemy climbs the rubble to the north and lines up a rocket launcher shot. If you aren't fast, he kills that lead tank in one shot. Shoot him before you do anything else.

Ideally, you're using your demolitions expert. Switch to your M136 and climb the rubble for a clear shot at the enemy tanks. When they're out of the way, stay low and keep yourself alive. Chip in where you can, but let your three tanks do the grunt work.

The enemy is well hidden in the university alcoves.

Should you have to do some work yourself, watch out for the enemy's crossfire trap. Five enemies hidden in the alcoves to the north, and three to the south, zing you from both directions. If you stray too far into the university courtyard, three enemies from down the street (northwest of your current position) will join the fight. Use your tanks; they have thicker hides than you do. It doesn't take long to achieve objective #1.

21-GUN SALUTE

Bravo's members have been asleep to this point; now you need them to wake up. From the insertion zone, run up the street and cut in where the destroyed tank lies smoldering. Head for the alley to your right, and follow it as a back door into Presidential Square. Before you reach the alley's end, you see an enemy tank sticking out. Arm your demo expert with his M136 and launch away. With any luck, you'll take one or two enemies with it.

From the alley, zap the enemy tank in Presidential Square.

TIP

Alleys between buildings provide shortcuts to surprise the enemy.

That leaves three or four enemies and a second enemy tank. Gun down the enemies first. Before the explosion, there are two enemies at the gates and two in the bunker to your left when you come out from the alley. Show no mercy and you should have them all in seconds. Even if the second enemy tank notices you and rotates to fire, there's ample cover, like the stone flag pole, which you can hide behind. When you're ready, step your demo guy in front of the blown-up tank to dismantle the second tank.

Presidential Square guards patrol in the street or near the iron gate.

When there's no enemy movement left in the square, objective #2 is yours. Wait here for the Alpha members to join up. They should be racing ahead of the tanks, and when they arrive, you're off again for the last objective point. If you don't think they can beat the tanks here, send Bravo on its own to the next checkpoint.

Take out the second tank before it has a chance to shoot.

STREETWISE

Only 13 more soldiers to go till you reach your final destination. This next part of the mission takes you through the Village Square and City Park on the way to the cathedral (objective #3). Only one soldier has a rocket launcher, so take things as slow as the tanks will allow.

Surprise the guards who congregate around the road divider in the Village Square.

Two enemies infest the Village Square, the next major intersection west of Presidential Square. Run your teams along the building fronts and take advantage of any alcove for cover. Peek around the corner and identify where the enemies set up. They are near the center of the intersection, walking around the road divider. Don't hang out too long—kill them or run to the park and let the tank deal with them.

Get your crosshairs on the final rocket launcher fast.

It's not till the park that you have to worry about the last rocket launcher. Six soldiers lie in ambush, ready to assault either road that merges into the park. The enemies are all over the place, though a clump of them waits to the north with others to the east. The soldier armed with the rocket launcher is to the east. Before you leave this area, take a headcount. If you don't come up with six, scour the area for the enemy so you can assure no missiles get fired.

While your attention is on the rocket launcher in the park, don't lose sight of the enemies to your left.

One two-man patrol stands in your way to the cathedral. The men wandering the northernmost road, just before the cathedral courtyard, don't pose a threat unless you're careless.

From the protection of the street corner, mow down the two-man patrol stopping you from reaching the cathedral.

HOLY WAR

The final confrontation pits you against six enemies and four tanks. When you hit the corner leading into the cathedral courtyard, take a quick scan of the surroundings. To your left, is a bunker and a tank. Don't worry about the tank; it doesn't fire at you right away. Across the courtyard, you see three more tanks, and nearby out of sight is a second bunker (in the same position as the first bunker, but on the other side). The steps in front of the cathedral hold most of the guards.

Three important targets in the courtyard are the enemy bunker, the nearest tank, and the cathedral steps.

From the corner, snipe the first bunker guard. Use your demo expert to shoot tanks one by one, starting with the one closest to the machine gun nest. Blow up a tank for each rocket you have left.

When you're out of missiles, head for the nearest bunker, sight extended, and shoot at any enemy that pops his head up. Position yourself on the bunker's side for cover. From there, take out the far bunker or whoever is raining fire on you. When the far bunker falls, it's easy to sidestep so the cathedral pillars aren't in your way, and cultivate a straight shot on the last four soldiers.

Trade fire between the far enemy bunker and the cathedral steps' pillars.

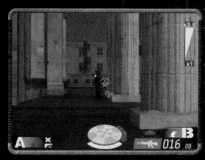

If these are the last of the enemies on the mission, you win. If not, get out your rocket launcher and have at the last couple of enemy tanks so your allied tanks can cruise to the finish line.

GR MISSION 11: DREAM KNIFE

Senators have power. And when a senator's son ends up a prisoner of war in a Russian camp, you can bet there's going to be a search and rescue attempt. Without raising the alarm, you need to sneak into the Ljady P.O.W. camp and retrieve three men unharmed. Start screwing on those silencers.

LEGEND

- **Number of Enemies at Location (PS2)**
- **Number of Enemies at Location (GameCube)**
- **Objective Number**
- **Stop Points**
- **Extraction Zone**
- **Insertion Zone**

MISSION CONDITIONS

Mission Name:	*GR M11 Dream Knife*
Location:	*Ljady, Russia*
Date:	*09/16/08*
Time:	*03:00*
Weather:	*Clear (night)*
Item Requirements:	*Silenced weapons*
Hidden Soldier:	*Dieter Munz, support (Weapon 7, Stealth 6, Endurance 5, Leadership 3, armed with an MG3 Light Machine Gun)*

OBJECTIVES

1. *Secure an Entrance*
2. *Rescue NATO POWs*
3. *Go to Extraction Zone*
X. *Rescue Moroshkin*

SEARCHING HIGH AND LOW

It's another night mission, and Night vision goggles are a must; but you have to take them off for the first few minutes of the mission.

Without night vision, you can't detect the enemy.

Before you tackle the camp guards, you first have to outmaneuver the searchlights. With night vision goggles on, it's difficult to see the searchlights on the ground. Put your goggles on after you reach the prison wall.

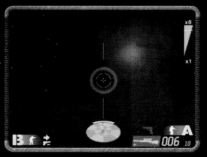

Freeze when the prison spotlight points at you. When it moves away, bolt for the prison wall.

Head south to the halfway point between the first entrance and the corner tower with the searchlight. Don't go so far that the guards can see you, but far enough past the tower that its searchlight has a tough time scanning over you. Time your run. Wait until the searchlight starts to swing back to the left, then run to the prison wall. You may have to angle so your two Alpha teammates don't stick out from the wall.

Trigger the alarm, and all the guards in the prison retreat to form a formidable perimeter around the P.O.W.s.

The alarm is sounded if the searchlight or guards spot you. Don't shoot out a spotlight—that sounds the alarm. If your team is detected, the alarm goes off seven seconds later. Now you're in for a major battle—all the enemies take up defensive positions around the hostages. If you sound the alarm on your escape, all the guards pour out to the north and try to prevent you from reaching the extraction zone.

CRASHING THE GATES

You can enter the complex from two different gates. Use the second one to the south, but stop by the first and visit those guards on the way. At this point, make sure your weapons all have silencers, like an MP5-SD or an M9SD.

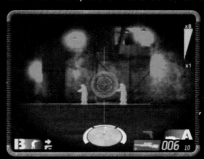

Clear out the guards at the first entrance so you don't have to deal with them on the return trip.

TIP

The sniper's rifle has a greater range than his pistol. To gain the range of the rifle with your pistol, zoom in on an enemy with the rifle, then toggle to the pistol without moving. If the enemy hasn't moved either, your pistol will be lined up with the perfect shot.

At the end of each road, there's a guardhouse—one opposite the prison entrance and one near the eastern map border. Each guardhouse holds two enemies. You can bypass these guardhouses by staying clear, but sometimes the extra enemies are drawn into a firefight. The guards from the southeast range out and search the woods, so don't let them surprise you on the trip to the second prison entrance.

The guardhouse enemies patrol the perimeter, so don't get too close.

As with the first entrance, the second entrance has three guards at the gate and two upstairs in the tower. You can creep in as far as the shadows outside the streetlight. Time your assault so that all three guards are close together, and do not shoot if there is an enemy patrol in the background *inside* the compound. If another patrol spots you, it will sound the alarm, and you'll have a mess on your hands. The same is true for one of the patrol guards; he's a "runner" and will run for the tower door when the firing begins to alert others. You must stop him to maintain secrecy on this mission.

Remove the three-man patrol in front of the gate, then zero in on the two guards in the tower.

If your troops are good with their MP5-SDs, take out the guards in the tower from outside the prison. Most likely, you'll need to sneak in and silence them. Slide up the stairs and get the drop on both guards before they can use their machine guns on you.

Sneak up the tower stairs to snipe the machine gunner.

DOCTOR APPOINTMENT

You're now inside. To the north, the main bulk of enemies defends the P.O.W.s. Head to the west and hope to avoid a major confrontation. From the tower door, scan the courtyard and deal with any enemies that show up. A two-man or three-man patrol is sometimes right outside the door.

Three guards sometimes patrol the courtyard outside the infirmary.

CAUTION

Be careful in this mission. The prisoners are always next to guards, and one stray bullet could kill them.

When the coast is clear, rush across the courtyard to the infirmary. Two guards hold Moroshkin hostage at gunpoint. Slide over to the main doorway until you have a clear shot at the first guard. Don't miss. Moroshkin stands behind the guard. Immediately sidestep into the room and blast the second guard behind the curtains to the north. With those two down, you have rescued Moroshkin and achieved the special objective—so long as he stays alive for the rest of the mission.

Kill the two infirmary guards and rescue Moroshkin to fulfill the mission's special objective.

Hide from the patrols on the road and ambush them from behind.

You need precision marksmanship for the next part of the mission. Outside the chain-link fence surrounding the P.O.W.s, drop prone and watch the guards' route. Don't open fire on them with the hostages standing in the middle; wait till the two guards stop and chat on one side. When they separate from the prisoners, quickly take your shot.

COMPLEX MANEUVERS

Head into the prison complex and watch for guards. Take cover alongside the two barracks to the north, always mindful of searching eyes. You can find a patrol on the main road or to the northwest by the P.O.W. pen. Hide from any patrol on the road; it's too easy for them to rally the rest of the complex guards. Instead, hit the patrol when it circles the barracks. Take out the patrol when it cuts between the barracks with an ambush at the corner, or when its members have their backs turned near the clothesline.

Careful where you aim in the P.O.W. pen. Shoot precisely and you free the prisoner.

Enemies swarm the east and northeast section of this compound. The alarm should not sound if you've been stealthy, which makes retreating easier. Secure the two P.O.W.s and retrace your steps. Watch for enemies who might show up along the chain-link fence or to the east in the main courtyard. Don't shoot at them; just run for the hills.

Think of yourself as a schoolteacher on the retreat. The A.I. that controls the two P.O.W.s and Moroshkin isn't the brightest. The prisoners can get stuck on building corners, in stairwells, and sometimes they just lose you. Proceed quickly so the enemy doesn't catch you, but stop at defensible positions and double-check to make sure everyone is still together. If you lose a prisoner, he might be difficult to find (or worse, dead), and you'll have to restart the mission.

Check that all prisoners are with you at safe locations.

If Bravo picks off a patrol, you won't run into a hassle on the return trip. The only danger could be the western side of the complex, since none of your soldiers have ventured near it. Even so, it should be quiet there. Escort the prisoners to the extraction zone and you've made a senator happy and added a political ally for life.

Enemies can show up anywhere along the chain-link fence or in the main courtyard to the east.

As you retreat, send Bravo due west of the insertion zone to the extraction zone. There are two three-man patrols that circle the outside of the complex. In addition to the guards circulating inside the compound, you detect these outside patrols as well. Unless you're lucky, they will intercept you. Set up Bravo on the woody perimeter in front of the extraction zone to kill any hostiles trying to stop you from reaching the extraction zone.

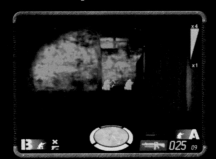

There are still a dozen guards left to stop your escape.

CAUTION

Remember, a prisoner follows the soldier who rescued him. Should the soldier die, you must "run into" the prisoner with a new soldier to have him follow you again.

GR MISSION 12: IVORY HORN

On the docks, you have to sink some ships. In a night raid on a Russian naval base, you must destroy a submarine and some fuel tanks to throw the military strength of the Ultranationalists in chaos. With your help, the Russian warmongering will soon be over.

A Russian naval base can't stand up long against your rifles and grenades.

LEGEND

- Number of Enemies at Location (PS2)
- Number of Enemies at Location (GameCube)
- Objective Number
- Stop Points
- Extraction Zone
- Insertion Zone

MISSION CONDITIONS

Mission Name: *GR M12 Ivory Horn*

Location: *Murmansk, Russia*

Date: *09/22/08*

Time: *02:00*

Weather: *Clear (night)*

Item Requirements: *Demo charges*

Hidden Soldier: *Astra Galinsky, sniper (Weapon 7, Stealth 7, Endurance 4, Leadership 2, armed with an M82A1)*

OBJECTIVES

1. *Plant Demo in Sub Pen 51*
2. *Plant Demo in Sub Pen 52*
3. *Get to Extraction Zone*
X. *Plant Demo in Fuel Depot*

WHAT'S UP DOCK?

You get it from both sides straight out of the insertion zone. Three enemy soldiers patrol the north part of the docks, while five Russians safeguard the Corvette. You can't waltz past the either patrol without arousing suspicion, so to break out the weaponry.

The Corvette enemies fire a few rounds and follow with a ground assault.

Keep your attention divided between the three-man patrol on the left and the five Corvette guards to the right.

TIP

Don't worry about stealth in this mission; the deck's so big that most enemies can't hear what's going on unless it's in their immediate area.

The insertion zone starts you *below* the main dock, which gives you a significant cover advantage. Choose someone, preferably with a machine gun or a sniper rifle, to pick off the three-man patrol at long distance, and climb the initial ramp until your gun tip rests flush on the dock.

The five soldiers on the Corvette are hard to spot, so start with the three-man patrol when its route comes closest to you. Shoot the patrollers then swing back to the right side and focus on the soldiers pouring off the Corvette. A favorite tactic of those five is to lob a grenade in the air, then charge at you in all the commotion. One of them sprays the docks with machine gun fire, so be on the lookout for him. You may have to dance around the crates cluttering the dockyard, but eventually the enemy will fall.

When you think the coast is clear, head for Objective #1, the first sub pen. Unlike the second underground sub pen, the sub is right there at the edge of the docks ready to be blown sky high. You have three charges and three targets, so don't miss.

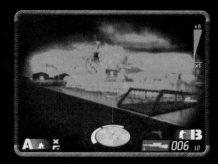

Plant your demo charge and blast a hole in objective #1.

20
30
40
50
60
70
80
90
00
10
20
30
40
50
60
70

> **TIP**
> Take two demolitions experts on this mission so you have double the demo charges.

FIRE FOR THE FUEL

Two patrols near the cargo holds carry grenade launchers.

There are three free-floating guards in the map's center, patrolling around the office parking lot. Discretion is the better part of valor here. If you think you can snipe them without bringing others to the rescue, remove the threat so you don't have to deal with it later. Otherwise, pass by quietly and you may not see them on the return trip.

Three enemies near the fuel tanks have no idea you're coming.

The assault point for the fuel tanks lies to the southwest. Three guards watch the entry ramp, one in the booth to the left and two walking the chain-link fence. Go prone at the range of your scope and crawl in for a better shot. Hit the two outside first. The one inside the booth is a tougher shot, and you don't want the other two to draw a bead on you while you're trying to pinpoint the booth guard.

When you blow these fuel tanks, the Russian Ultranationalists can't even run their mopeds.

Under the fuel tanks, patience should be your watchword. It's easy for the enemy to sneak up the ramp on the eastern side and catch you unaware. It's difficult to see when you're standing or crouching. The best game plan is to go prone at the western end and wait for signs of movement. There are four enemies who defend the fuel tanks, though generally they are split apart into two-man teams. Look for two to approach the tanks, and have your sniper deal with them. The second team should be close behind.

The guards at the fuel tank usually patrol in two teams.

SUBMARINE SANDWICH

Most of the dock's eastern side should be deserted now. Of course, that should set off alarm bells in your head—something can't be right.

The enemy has two ambushes planned for you: one in the underground complex that houses the submarine, and the other on your retreat back to the extraction zone. Eliminate the second one on the way to the first.

The more enemies you kill heading into the submarine hangar, the less you have to deal with later.

Before you reach the submarine complex, there's a building to the south that holds radioactive material (presumably for the sub's reactor). The radiation isn't harmful, but the four guards preparing to ambush you are. If an alarm goes off on the docks, these four, along with the four enemies in the office building, sweep onto the docks and blast everything in sight. Ambush them before they can tag team you.

The tunnel to the sub can be a deathtrap if you're not fast in close combat.

The next entrance to the north is the submarine tunnel. Wind down and prepare for a big fight. Eight guards surround your position, and it's difficult to see them through the metal grating and tight spaces. You have to move fast.

Submarine guards are crawling all over the place.

TIP

Inside the submarine hangar, and in any close-combat fight, don't zoom; you lose too much of your peripheral vision.

Arm yourself with a quick weapon, like the M16, and turn to the right. Don't linger in the doorway; someone will shoot at you. There is no initial enemy to your left, so take care of business on the right side. Two guards come at you, and more follow. They can easily gain access from the steel catwalk above. Take them down and move into a defensive position in the right corner behind the wall's thick cover.

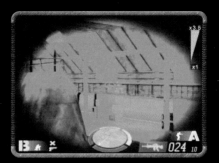

A four-man ambush sets up outside the submarine tunnel.

After the initial shootout, send Bravo to flush out the enemy.

The ambush files out of the building to the southwest. The enemy spreads out fast and tries to mow you down or shoot a grenade into your middle. Get your whole team outside, then drop prone so everyone can shoot (pull Bravo out too if you have time). If you're good, you can plug all the enemies and not take a shred of shrapnel.

MISSION STATUS

Not every mission ends in a complete success. You can always restart until you get your orders perfect; however, sometimes you just want to move on. That could be the case after the submarine showdown. It's brutal, and you might have to lose a guy to escape. It's not the end of the world—you've only got three missions to go—and there's the consolation that your soldier gave his life for a noble cause.

At this point, bring team Bravo down for added support and to flush out the enemy. When Bravo enters, move Alpha along the perimeter or climb the nearest ladder. If Bravo doesn't find the enemy quickly, you will as you circle for a better shot.

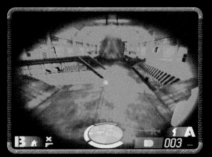

The submarine complex is anything but simple.

Your threat indicator eventually turns blue, and you can call upon a demo expert to plant the final charge on the sub. That destroys the sub and completes objective #2, and also sets off the dock alarms. There's one last test ahead.

HALF AN AMBUSH

You have to face four more enemies on the way home, since you've already killed half of the ambush party before the visit to the submarine hangar.

When you exit the submarine hangar, glance to your right to locate two guards who patrol that northern dock wing. You should have picked them off on your way south, or on your way to the sub, and don't have to worry about them now. If not, don't let them get a good shot while you face the four ahead.

GR MISSION 13: ARCTIC SUN

"Hit them hard and fast and get out as quickly as possible." According to your commanding officer, that's the best way to approach this mission, and who's going to argue? Your job is to destroy a new experimental fighter prototype, the S37 Berkut, as well as Russia's latest attack helicopter, the Ka50 Hokum. Just because your intelligence reports say it's lightly guarded doesn't mean you shouldn't pack backup frags.

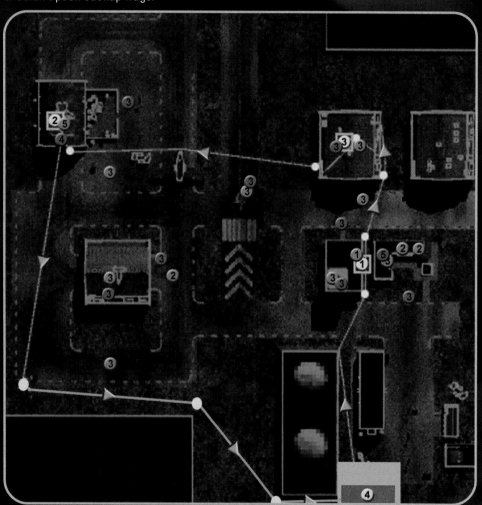

LEGEND

- Number of Enemies at Location (PS2)
- Number of Enemies at Location (GameCube)
- Objective Number
- Stop Points
- Extraction Zone
- Insertion Zone

MISSION CONDITIONS

Mission Name: *GR M13 Arctic Sun*

Location: *Arkhangel'sk, Russia*

Date: *10/03/08*

OBJECTIVES

1. *Secure Control Tower*

2. *Destroy S37 Berkut*

3. *Destroy KA-50 Hokum*

It's not another naval base. This time you're on an airbase to destroy planes and copters.

WIPE OUT THE TOWER

You have three targets, the first of which is the control tower, and they all have to blow within about five minutes of each other.

You eventually head due north to the control tower building. Still, you must always be mindful of the enemies around you in case they get uppity. To the distant east you see a firehouse. A two-man patrol walks the backyard (out of sight behind the firehouse) and patrols the buildings to the north. The two men can easily be avoided. However, if you want to eliminate their submachine guns, knock them off early, and then backtrack to the insertion zone area.

Two enemies hide out behind the firehouse.

As you head north, take a look northwest across the airfield. You will hit those targets later. In the meantime, watch where the enemies are congregating. This helps you plot a course when you visit the west side of the map; it can also reduce your chances of taking a wound. For example, don't open up on the enemy team patrolling the junction box if someone on the airfield can see you. That invites trouble.

Don't shoot anyone on the airfield until you've taken care of control tower.

A four-man patrol circles the office building and the control tower building. Don't mess with them. One shoots a machine gun, and another a grenade launcher. Bide your time until they pass the corner and begin their route up the street between the two buildings. Follow them carefully, and when you think you have a good shot at their tails, unload with everything you've got.

Take out the four-man patrol that guards the control tower from behind.

Assault Objective #1, the control tower, from the door on its east side. Search the building for its four enemies, but be very careful—they can jump out from open doorways or hit you from the stairs. Normally, you can find one bad guy in the office room on the first floor, and three in the control room upstairs.

Objective #1's door is located just before the junction box.

TIP

Don't get jumpy. Half the enemies on this map are inside buildings, so your threat indicator might be red without an immediate confrontation.

HOKUM HANGAR

Expect a guard at the door to this hangar to be armed with grenades. Take him out first, and then hang a right and head upstairs. At the top of the stairs, snipe the guard near the railing. He's not quick on the trigger and should go down fast.

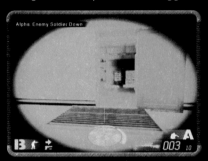

Your first targets in the Hokum hangar are the guards lying in ambush. Eliminate them and then take out the enemies around the plane.

Drop prone and start firing over the ledge. There should be three to four soldiers left on the ground floor, but they're tough. Each is armed with a carbine (instead of an assault rifle) and hand grenades to throw. Fortunately, it's a difficult throw to bounce it up on the balcony near the stairwell. Don't bother with your own frags—it's better to zoom and fire.

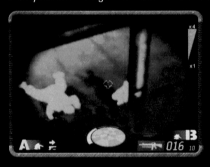

After you finish off the plane's immediate guards, watch out for a second team to arrive.

When the ground enemies fall, scour the second floor for two more enemies. Dodge around corners and shoot at any heat signature. Once the threat indicator turns blue, head downstairs and plant the explosive charge on the Hokum to complete objective #3.

You thought the encounter was over, right? Well, maybe if you hurry. Once you plant the demo charge on the Hokum, six enemies from the neighboring building rush into the hangar to reinforce. You have a choice: fight or run.

Expect fierce reinforcements for the Hokum hangar after you plant the demolitions charge.

If you fight, it will be a big battle, so take up defensive positions around the hangar. You should leave at least one team on the second-story balcony and another behind whatever crates you find. You can catch many of the enemy in a crossfire this way.

CAUTION

The enemies on this mission secretly reinforce. Almost every building has hidden danger.

AIRSTRIP ASSAULT

If you run from the Hokum hangar, move quickly. You don't want reinforcements sniping at your back. Head to the hangar's western door and take defensive positions outside the building (prone and against the wall is fine).

Use your sniper to kill the airfield enemies to the southwest.

To your left, you have three or six enemies. Most likely, it's three. Three of the six are in a wandering patrol that helps out on the eastern side of the map. You might have already dealt with them when you attacked the four-man patrol by the junction box or the single guard outside the Hokum hangar. If this is the case, you have less to deal with now. If not, your sniper has to pull double duty.

Zoom in with your sniper for a head shot on the closest target. Repeat with the second two if possible. Hopefully, the rest of your guys have good shots and join in to make it quick. When the soldiers to the southwest fall, get up and book toward the plane in the middle of the field.

On the move, you have to knock out the four guards to the airstrip's north.

Be on guard here. Four hostiles patrol the northern section of the fields. You need to move toward them and take them down at the same time. Remember, six enemies are reinforcing behind you in the Hokum hangar (if you haven't killed them yet), and you don't want anyone shooting at you while you're vulnerable. The four should fall without much effort—there's very little cover for a successful retreat.

SECRET HANGAR

The last objective is the top secret S37 Berkut. The experimental Russian project is heavily guarded. Don't be fooled by the hangar's stillness when you first approach.

Guards surround the S37 Berkut and protect it with their lives.

Five soldiers defend the Berkut. They charge you, guns blazing. You might end up fighting the entire fight from the hangar doorway; they seldom give you a chance to do anything but fire. Keep your teams behind you, and use the doorframe as cover. Go prone the second you hear gunfire. By the end of the fight, if you haven't seen the whites of the enemy's eyes, you're an expert.

Machine gunners lie in wait inside Berkut hangar.

The Berkut is a beautiful, sleek craft, but it's got to go. Plant your last demo charge and finish objective #2. Now you must return to the extraction zone, but it won't be a cake walk.

ONE LAST TRAP

Four enemies in the hangar south of the Berkut hangar complicate things. Once you plant the charge on the Berkut, they take up defensive positions on the airfield and try to surprise you with a few shells to the head. Considering that two have grenade launchers and one a machine gun, that might be really bad.

The last ambush is on top of you before you know it.

TIP

Before a fight, always scan the arena for the best cover and use it.

Proceed cautiously out of the Berkut hangar, and scan for enemies to the south. The trick here is to identify where they're located. If you can zero in, you can either snipe them at long range or find some cover to shoot at them. Whatever you do, don't charge to the extraction zone until you've dealt with the ambush. You can't outrun them.

The two guards who seal off the extraction zone aren't a problem for your crack teams.

When the coast is clear, head south to the extraction zone. There should only be two soldiers guarding the zone. After what you've been through recently, you can mow them down with your eyes closed. Rest for a second, bandage your wounds, and be glad that you won't see another plane on your tour with the Ghosts.

MISSION 14: WILLOW BOW

The Ultranationalists have one large army left. In the hills of Toropec, the radical Russians have set up their big defensive stand. The Ghosts need to escort two Bradley tanks into the region, control three key strategic points in the mountains, and wipe out the military camp on the other side. If you can manage all that, you've broken the enemy's back.

LEGEND

- **Number of Enemies at Location (PS2)**
- **Number of Enemies at Location (GameCube)**
- **Objective Number**
- **Stop Points**
- ○ **Allied Troops**
- ◇ **Allied Tank**
- ■ **Insertion Zone**

MISSION CONDITIONS

Mission Name:	*M14 Willow Bow*
Location:	*Toropec, Russia*
Date:	*10/23/08*
Time:	*13:00*
Weather:	*Snow*
Item Requirements:	*None*
Hidden Soldier:	*None*

OBJECTIVES

1. *Take North Pass*
2. *Take South Pass*
3. *Take Top of the Hill*
X. *Neutralize Russian camp*

MOUNTAIN CLIMBING

As with mission 10, when you had to protect tanks in the streets of Vilnius, your job here is to safeguard the Bradley tanks up the mountain range. However, this time you take a more aggressive role and kill most of the hostiles before the tanks can sight them.

TIP

One tank is better than two on this mission. It's easier to protect one tank in the mountain passes.

Don't activate the south Bradley tank. It adds an incredible amount of support fire and it's nice to send into a nest of enemies and not have to do a lick. However, you've got to keep the pesky things from getting blown up. Since your troops kill the brunt of the enemies, it's a headache to keep track of the extra tank.

The Ghosts are backed up by Bradley tanks on this mission.

Your movement is through mountain passes. Keep Alpha and Bravo on opposite sides of these narrow passages. If an enemy shows up in the middle, you have an instant crossfire. By advancing on either side, you lessen the chance of being blind-sided by the enemy—one of your teams should spot them. For additional backup, swing Alpha or Bravo away from their sides to lend support fire.

You don't need to fight the three guards by the log cabin. Save your energy for the other hostiles on the map.

Should you charge up the southern pass and activate the south Bradley tank, you will quickly run into a log cabin. Three hostiles don't take kindly to strangers. They patrol their property's eastern edge, so you can frequently catch them at the building's corner. Unless you have an overwhelming compulsion to wipe out all enemies on the map, avoid this encounter.

HOUSE ON THE HILL

Head to the eastern pass and travel toward the north pass objective point. You don't hit resistance until you cut into the second gap. As you climb the hill, scan for three enemies on the plateau to your right. They might take a potshot at you from up high, but they prefer to hide in the trees and bushes and wait for you to head toward the north pass house. If he can, the one with the grenade launcher drops a frag into your team.

Three enemies on your way to the north pass try to hit you from behind.

Another enemy house sits at the top of the hill near the north pass objective. Two teams of two patrol the grounds. One team engages you at the corner of the house where it can take cover against a rocky outcropping. Deal with that, but also keep your eye on the second patrol. It either backs up the first patrol or circles around the house and hits you from the east.

The four enemies at the house tend to attack from the southwest corner.

Throughout all of this, one of the enemies on the top of the hill (objective #3) fires down on you with a sniper rifle. Don't proceed too far up the hill, you have to fight the four house enemies first. After they fall, you can turn your attention to the sniper on the hill.

Beware the sniper on the hill. He's a great shot.

Don't wander too far east (toward the low-lying rock wall), or you'll draw the north pass enemies into the fight. Just like the assassin on the hill, one member of the north pass two-man patrol has a sniper rifle, and you don't want to be pinned down between those two guys.

CAUTION

Never charge into a situation and activate all of the surrounding enemies. You don't want to fight everyone at once.

With all of this going on, a three-man patrol guarding the pass to the top of the hill comes down and reinforces the house enemies. One has a grenade launcher. He shoots several grenades if he has no fear of hitting his fellow comrades.

Finish off the last two-man team and the north pass is yours.

Assuming the house guards are dead, turn your attention to the hill sniper and pick him off with your sniper. Duck against the west side of the house and unload on the three-man patrol heading down to reinforce. After the three-man patrol falls, turn your attention to the second sniper. If you've managed to stay out of sight for a while, the two-man north pass team will get impatient and head down from its perch to try to outflank you in the north. Take cover by the rock walls or inside the house's stone porch and pick off the last two enemies.

You might take casualties here, but you will most likely fulfill two objectives at once, the top of the hill (objective #3) and the north pass (objective #1). If not, trudge up the hill and mop up the one or two enemies who remain. All of this craziness happens before the allied tank crests the north pass hill.

SURPRISE PARTY

Take a tip from the enemy snipers and abuse the top of the hill terrain. Since the enemy has two machine gun nests defending the pass, assault them from the eastern hilltop instead of tackling them head on.

Shoot the dangerous western machine gun nest before turning your attention to the lone guard in the eastern nest.

Head southwest from the top of the hill till you see the pipeline crossing the mountains. Follow the pipeline and you come to the cliff where you can shoot down on the enemy. Watch for a two-person patrol on the cliff opposite you; one of the guards has a sniper rifle that can easily reach you. Usually, these two come down from the hill and become your last targets.

The patrol near the south pass has a sniper.

Focus on the two machine gun nests. If you've crept to the cliff's edge, they might not have noticed you yet. Keep it that way till you've lined up the perfect sniper shot on the western machine gun nest (the one that can shoot back at you). Kill these two before turning your attention to the guard who mans the eastern machine gun nest. If you play it right, he can't line up a shot against you. Walk along the cliff until you hit him with a sniper blast. The second objective should trigger, and you're on your way to the Russian camp.

DEATH CAMP

The next two encounters have rocket launchers. If you don't remove them in a timely fashion, say goodbye to the Bradley tank.

Double back to the north pass and head south. On the far side of the big rock, two three-man patrols prepare for the coming tank. One of these patrols carries an antitank missile and climbs the rocks behind you to destroy the tank if you can't stop it.

Two patrols wait for the allied tank south of the north pass, and one of the enemy teams carries a rocket launcher.

It doesn't matter which team is which—wipe them both out with impunity. The second team, the one without the rocket launcher, uses a grenade launcher. That's not much fun, especially if the enemies can get some altitude on you and rain bombs from above. If you've followed this section's strategy from the beginning, you don't have to worry about your second Bradley tank being destroyed. It's important that these enemies be annihilated before moving to intercept any others.

To the west of the plateau above the enemy encampment lies a range of machine gun nests. To the south, you can see a shack and an enemy group. If it's a two-man group, it has the second rocket launcher. Kill that group first. A second enemy group, comprised of three guys, watches the pass to the west in hopes of taking your tank division off guard. If you see them, fire away.

Before you tackle the camp's machine gun nests, take out the enemy patrol by the shack. It has the second rocket launcher.

When there are no enemies in sight, head to the area with the shack. Two cautions here: first, the second enemy patrol could still be in the area; second, the machine gunner to the east is an amazing shot. To take the camp, you need to successfully navigate down to the rocks east of the shack and obtain a better shot on the machine gunner. Otherwise, he'll eat you alive.

The camp's machine gunner is the best enemy shooter in the game. You have to get closer to beat him.

When the area around the shack is clear, throw your team up against the east rocks and slide along to the south till you get a clear shot. The machine gunner has to die first, or your team won't be alive to hunt for any others. After he falls, snipe at the last four to close out the mission.

The remaining enemies try to stop you, but you need to get to the rocks near the Russian camp so you can wipe out the five soldiers manning the machine guns.

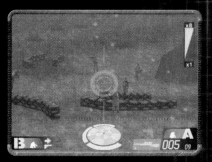

If you're having trouble, turn to your M203s or OICWs and arc some grenades over the hill. You'll either score kills or scatter the enemy away from their sandbags. After they're routed, you shouldn't have as much resistance. Capture objective #4 and you're on your way to Moscow.

Well-placed grenades always end the mission faster.

GR MISSION 15: WHITE RAZOR

You know things are bad for the Ultranationalists when your team sits in Moscow. Before you can take out the Kremlin, U.S. troops are pinned down by the enemy in the medieval quarter. Save their bacon, then stroll over to Red Square for the final battle.

Moscow's streets look quiet—
that's because you haven't seen
the tanks yet.

LEGEND

- ⊙ **Number of Enemies at Location (PS2)**
- ⊙ **Number of Enemies at Location (GameCube)**
- ❶ **Objective Number**
- ● **Stop Points**
- ○ **Allied Troops**
- ◼ **Insertion Zone**
- ⊤ **Tank**

MISSION CONDITIONS

Mission Name: *GR M15 White Razor*

OBJECTIVES

1. *Relieve Pinned-Down Troops*

RUSSIA IN THE WINTERTIME

The first half of this mission is no more challenging than basic training. The hardest part is holding back from plugging a civilian so you can complete objective #4. You can combat as few as five enemies before the grand finale, which is good. You need to conserve your strength.

With the element of surprise on your side, the first enemy patrol doesn't have a prayer.

Head southeast to save the U.S. troops. Only one patrol—three men armed with a machine gun, grenade launcher, and semiauto—stands in your way. They traverse the south street behind the apartment buildings. Cut down the street after the second building and watch for the patrol at the corner. Drop prone as soon as you catch a glimpse of them. It's tough for the enemies to find cover, other than some partial protection in doorways, so they should drop without Alpha or Bravo taking a slug. If they don't show up right away, move on; you don't want to waste too much time waiting for them to show. You have allied troops to save.

CAUTION

Russian civilians run in front of you, even during a firefight. Watch who you shoot.

Wind through the streets till you reach the large park. Don't bother trying to pick off enemies from long range. They are invulnerable (as are the U.S. troops) until you pass the trigger point about halfway down the last street leading into the large park.

Shoot the Russians, not the Americans.

Once you cross the vulnerability threshold, gun down the enemies quickly before they get a chance to use their machine guns. Snipe the two in the plaza, then run for the eastern firefight (objective #1). The U.S. troops are effective and may wipe out a Russian or two on their own, but they need your help fast to survive.

TO RED SQUARE

There should be an entrance inside the mall to the south. Take it, but watch out for civilians who dart out of the mall directly in your path. You don't want to blast one by accident.

Be careful of Russian citizens who like to behave like enemy soldiers.

Inside the mall, you have two patrols to worry about. The first is just inside the main archway to your right. Three enemies shoot at you as soon as you turn the corner. Swing around, guns blazing, or drop prone and pick them off before they can target you. After those three fall, there are two guards on the catwalk immediately above you. Don't move forward until you drop those two.

Since the mall has a giant crack running through it, you only have one choice—the stairs to the second level. There is a second three-man patrol guarding the exit to Red Square, so come upon them quickly and quietly.

Polish up the last two patrols before Red Square. From here on out, it's no picnic.

GREMLINS IN THE KREMLIN

You're about to throw a monkey wrench into the Ultranationalists' remaining hardware. One last run through the tanks and machine guns fortifying Red Square, and you can retire permanently.

At long last, you've made it to Moscow's Red Square.

Switch to your demolitions expert and get both Alpha and Bravo ready to go in the small alcove. A lot happens before you even look out across Red Square. Be prepared to do things in rapid-fire order.

First, turn the corner with your demo expert and drop prone. Make sure the rest of Alpha is out in the street with you. Do the same for Bravo, sticking as close to the wall as you can. Eventually, you see a tank—the first of two you must destroy.

You must destroy the Nikoskaya tank before you can proceed into Red Square.

Second, a band of three or more enemies charges around the corner. There are seven floating enemies on the west side of the square, and many of them engage you on this street. Stay put and clip as many as you can as they round the corner.

Hit the Russians when they round the Red Square corner.

Third, switch to your antitank missile when the enemy tank turns in your direction. With all the destruction at the corner, the tank changes its direction to rain some shells on your teams. As soon as it does, your demo expert's priority is to take out that tank. Let your other five soldiers cover you if any other enemies show up.

Rise to a crouch and prepare your antitank missile when the enemy tank turns in your direction.

Fourth, launch the missile and don't miss. It's death for you if that tank shoots back. Odds are you won't get a second missile off with all the other firing that's going on.

Kill the second tank, or it kills you.

Inch your teams into the street and widen their arcs of fire into Red Square. They support you as you head to the corner and take out the machine gun nest to the south.

Your sniper can pop enemies across the square if you give her the shot.

Move to the corner, but don't expose yourself to the main section of the square yet. You need to cut down the machine gunner straight ahead, or he'll mow down your whole squad. Waste a whole clip on him if you have to—whatever it takes to knock him down fast. If you don't, expect heavy resistance to round that corner again.

Take out the first machine gun and expect the rest of the Nikoskaya Tower guards to jump all over you.

Once the machine gun nest empties, bring both Alpha and Bravo up to the corner. There should be minimal resistance left, except for another tank heading your way soon. Launch a missile into the second tank, and objective #1 should be yours.

When the last of the seven enemies on the west side of Red Square drops, you have taken Nikoskaya Tower.

Cut across the courtyard, past the demolished bus, and head for the giant debris pile directly in the center. You have many different enemy targets to worry about. Two machine gun posts lie to the southeast. To the south, a three-man patrol talks beside a brick wall. Far back in the eastern section of the square, the third enemy tank cruises with a five-man escort. All the enemy teams come equipped with a wide variety of hand grenades, grenade launchers, and submachine guns.

On the east side of Red Square, the two-man patrol closest to the mounted machine gun goes first.

Drop the two-man patrol near the center rubble pile. If the patrol reaches the mounted machine guns nearby, look out. When you kill one soldier, the guards by the brick wall to the south become alerted and take up defensive positions. Grenades work wonders here, as does the sniper, if you have a little extra time.

Don't let the three-man patrol zero in on where you are.

TIP

Include two demolitions experts with M136s in your outfit. To complete this mission, you must eliminate both enemy tanks.

After you've dealt with the five by the machine gun nest, scan around the center debris. If another patrol hears gunfire, it will join the party. Shoot anyone who tries to man the machine gun, then send Bravo up to the next debris pile. Keep spread out in case of grenades, and work your tag team magic on the enemy. There should be less than half-a-dozen soldiers defending the square at this point. Set them up for a crossfire and you're home free.

The last soldiers try to steal victory away from you.

The only thing stopping you at this point is a dead demolitions expert. During the heavy firefighting, keep at least one demo guy out of harm's way. Imagine your frustration if you blow apart all 17 enemies in Red Square and come up short because you don't have a rocket left. With the enemy soldiers wiped out, you have the luxury of lining up a picturesque shot.

As the last tank falls, so do the Ultranationalists.

MISSION IMPROBABLE

Group hug time. You've accomplished the next-to-impossible and succeeded at 15 different covert missions with the odds stacked incredibly against you. Enjoy your well-earned vacation. Unless there's another political disaster—another warlord invasion, say, in Africa—the American people probably won't need you for a while.

DS MISSION 1: BURNING SANDS

There's no place like the beach—except when you're stuck in the freezing water, it's 3:00 in the morning, and there are dozens of gun-slinging guerrillas combing the sand. Your mission as a Special Forces soldier is to ignore all these factors and concentrate on your targets. Tonight, you must wax two different enemy encampments, a radio tower and twin machine gun nests.

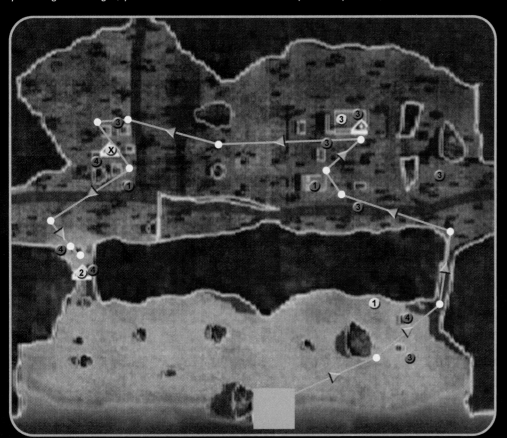

LEGEND

- ① **Number of Enemies at Location**
- ❶ **Objective Number**
- ● **Stop Points**
- ■ **Insertion Zone**

MISSION CONDITIONS

Mission Name:	*DS M1 Burning Sands*
Location:	*Samhar Awraja, Eritrea*
Date:	*05/16/09*
Time:	*3:00*
Weather:	*Clear*
Item Requirements:	*None*

OBJECTIVES

1. *Eliminate Beach Encampment*
2. *Neutralize Machine Guns*
3. *Secure Area Around Radio Tower*
X. *Eliminate Main Tent Zamp*

BEACH PARTY

Your first task is to pick off the enemy encampment on the beach. Head northeast from your starting position, toward the giant rock on the beach. This is your anchor point. If you come directly at the rock from the water, the enemy can't see you.

From the cover of the rock, flank team Alpha to the left. Go prone and crawl until you draw a bead on the first group of three. Make sure you tell Alpha to hold their fire, or they'll start shooting while you get Bravo ready.

Team Bravo fans right and drops prone to take aim on the second enemy team. The idea is to hit both groups at the same time to keep return fire to a minimum.

Using the protection of the beach's giant rock, one of your fireteams engages your first objective.

When you think you're done, you're not. Wait until the "objective complete" window pops up. If it doesn't, it means there's another mercenary out there. The enemy's favorite hiding spots are behind the palm tree to the west of the tents, or behind the eastern tent. If you walk into the campfire light too soon, you'll take one to the head.

Expose yourself to the firelight too soon, and the hidden mercenary will put another notch on his belt.

From this point, head up the eastern trail to the top of the hill. If you move fairly quickly, you won't have any problems. Hang out on the beach too long, and the nearest three-man group from the radio tower area will come down here on patrol. Prepare for unexpected company should you waste too much time on the beach.

TIP

It's a night mission, so use night vision goggles. In some areas, like around campfires and inside buildings where light's intense, you need to take them off.

RADIO DAYS

At the top of the hill, use the small rock to your left as another barrier. If you haven't already done so, switch to your sniper and nestle him up against the rock looking at the buildings to the west. Make sure his arc of fire covers the buildings, the radio tower, and the hill to the east. From here, you have command of the whole battlefield.

You may not kill all the enemies near the western buildings. Take out as many as you can to make your rifleman's upcoming charge less dangerous.

Start with the two or three guys milling about between the western buildings. Even at 8x sight range, it's a long shot. You have the element of surprise, though, and should snipe at least two before giving up your position.

Your sniper is better than the enemy's, primarily because you're hidden and he's not.

Scan to your right to pick up the enemy sniper on the radio tower's rooftop. He has a mean shot if you let him, so don't. Sniper on sniper, you know where he is, and that's all the difference. One shot should be enough.

Don't let the enemy surprise you from your blind side.

Your last sniper target is the three-man group on the hill. If you wait too long, they'll hear all the gunshots and descend on you like stealth bombers. Don't let them get the drop on you, especially from your blind side between the rock and the hill. If you have time, snipe all three of them with your long-range shooter. If you take too much time with the first two engagements, switch to a rifleman and have him scour the hill from the backside of the rock. You may have to ferret out one or two of them if you shoot the first guy and the others hide.

CAUTION

If you miss an enemy, be careful he doesn't sneak around buildings and trees and cap you from behind.

With sniper support, one of your riflemen charges the guards patrolling the radio tower yard.

Your sniper's roll is now support, as you need to take charge of a rifleman and clean up the remaining guards on the radio tower grounds. If you follow the rock wall in front of the buildings, there's a man hidden in the first shack to your right and one at the tree (provided your expert sniper hasn't plugged 'em already). Mow these guys down, then drop on the other side of the tree for a clear shot north at the three guards walking the perimeter of the radio tower.

The last guard before the radio tower is an easy mark in the corner of the westernmost building.

If you've shelled the enemy properly, there are only two guards left. The westernmost building has a single door you can open. Immediately inside, an enemy "guards" a stack of chairs on a table. He's an easy mark if you fire as you open the door.

Watch the guard at the radio tower window. He's waiting to kill whoever touches the doorknob.

The last enemy preventing objective #3's completion lies in ambush by the door to the radio tower house. He's waiting to kill the first soldier who touches the door. Shake him up and rain lead through the window. While he ducks for cover, open the door and slide inside for a direct shot at the disoriented mercenary. Congratulations. You've disabled the radio tower without cutting a single wire.

TENT HUT

The enemy on the guard tower is your priority target because he is the closest to you.

Once you silence the radio tower, head up the hill to the west. You have a grand view of the entire enemy tent encampment at the top. If you come up in the middle, to your left is a guard tower. To your right is a string of three tents with guards wandering about. Over to the far left, the two machine gun nests (objective #2) point toward the south. Incidentally, that's why you've come up the "back door." It'd be suicide to charge up the beach from the south and hit a pair of fortified bunkers with machine guns cross-haired on your nose.

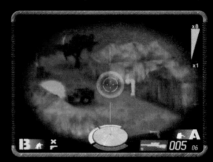

In all the confusion, it takes a few seconds for your enemies to figure out you're sniping at them from the hill. Use that time to nail anyone out in the open.

Switching back to sniper mode, set your sights on the guard in the tower directly ahead. He's the closest, so he's gotta go first. After you shoot, everyone else runs for cover. They haven't identified where you are yet, so take advantage and pick off a couple of guys during the confusion. As soon as the bullets start zinging past your head, direct your attention to the enemy who seems to be coming the closest. That enemy is the next to go.

Whatever you do, avoid shooting toward the southwest where the machine gunners lie in wait. The A.I. won't recognize your current gunfight, so those enemies won't activate yet. You have enough on your hands just tracking down the tent camp enemies who are waiting for you to come down and visit.

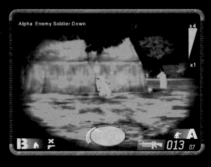

Inevitably, some of the enemies hide behind the northwest tent, and you have to track them down for the mission objective.

NEST OF VIPERS

From the safety of the downed tent camp, it's finally time to eliminate the machine gun nests—from behind.

After the last guard falls in the tent camp, circle around the guard tower and find another rock—they've become your best friends. With the nearby rock as cover, drop prone and scope in on the southern machine gun nest. You see the tops of the enemies' heads above the hill line. One shot is probably all you'll get before they duck for cover. The second machine gun team to your right is an even tougher shot since it has trees in the way. Be patient. They pop their heads up like ducks in a shooting gallery.

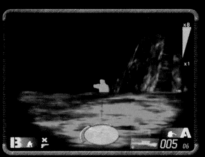

Guards from the second machine gun nest abandon their post and try to flank you. Zero in on them as they emerge from the palm trees.

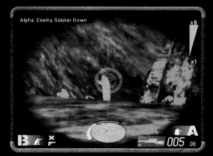

When the shooting dies down—the enemy may be bunkered in their nests—switch from the sniper to the rifleman and run to the north. Follow the border west to come up on the machine gun nest over the hill. Most of the guys should be dead from your sniper, so resistance is minimal. Don't hesitate—charge for the bunker and blow away anything that moves.

Hopefully, sniper fire has driven the enemies out of their bunker for easy kills.

With the first bunker finished, hug the rock that divides the bunkers and hold the trigger down as you round the corner. The hardest enemy is entrenched behind the sandbags. If you're fast, you'll get close enough to say lights out.

The mission ends when you finish off the last bunker crew.

Take a nice, long breath and relax. The mission's a success, and you've hardly broken a sweat. Just wait. The tough ones are yet to come.

DS MISSION 2: FLAME PILLAR

Usually, you're the one blowing up stuff. This time around, the enemy wants to destroy a refinery, and it's your job to stop it. It won't be easy. These guys aren't fooling around. If you want to keep the refinery in one peace, quickly eliminate enemies and drive for the detonation site. On the way home, as a token of appreciation for the locals, you'll rescue three Eritrean workers. Maybe you can be home in time for dinner?

LEGEND

- ❶ **Number of Enemies at Location**
- ❶ **Objective Number**
- ● **Stop Points**
- ■ **Extraction Zone**
- ■ **Insertion Zone**

MISSION CONDITIONS

Mission Name: *DS M2 Flaming Pillar*

Location: *Massawa, Eritrea*

Date: *05/23/09*

Time: *11:00*

Weather: *Sunny*

Item Requirements: *None*

OBJECTIVES

1. *Eliminate Explosives Squad*

2. *Rescue Captive Workers*

3. *Reach Extraction Zone*

X. *Eliminate all Enemy Units*

JEEPERS CREEPERS

A stone's throw from the insertion zone, the enemy guards the road in force.

Flick off your safeties immediately. Five seconds into this mission, you have a fight on your hands. Five enemies lie in wait on the road and around the rocks just in front of the insertion zone. It's hard to count them all in the heat of the moment, but it goes something like this: A three-man team patrols the road and frequently ducks behind the rock outcropping on the west end of the road. One solo mercenary drives a jeep packed with explosives, probably meant for the refinery or another similar target. The last loner hangs near the big western rock and doesn't peek out until you've engaged his partners.

A bullet plus an explosive-laden jeep equal one dead Ethiopian soldier.

Aim for the three-man group first. You'll do more damage concentrating on three than chasing after one. Ambush them before they disappear behind the rock. Next, the jeep driver heads toward you, slams on the brakes, and cocks his rifle to fire. Rip a few bullets in his direction and watch the fireworks. Loaded with explosives, his jeep erupts like a solar flare. Remember this when you're in the hangar trying to rescue the prisoners.

Watch your back, or the fifth member of the first enemy squad plugs you from behind the rocks.

To the west, the last enemy hides behind the big rock. If you run straight for the refinery, he will no doubt kill the first soldier to enter his arc of fire. Instead, circle your troops around the rock and flush him out. Six on one shouldn't be a problem.

Good job. You've prevented a truck full of explosives from reaching the refinery. The only problem is the demolitions expert is already setting the charges.

REFINED QUALITY

A sniper and a rifleman watch the eastern refinery entrance and try to buy time for their demo expert.

When you have five dead on the road, head straight for the refinery. You can enter at a number of points, but it's best to run all the way down and insert from the main road entrance. From here, you can catch the sniper off guard. He lies prone waiting for someone to enter from the eastern entrance, where he has a clean head shot. Shoot the sniper first, then press forward.

TIP

It's difficult to run two teams inside the refinery. The enclosed spaces don't allow for crossfires. Use one team and leave the other one safe outside to back you up if need be.

The demo expert plants his charge. Another few seconds and the refinery will be history.

Enemy patrols could be around any cylinder inside the refinery compound.

A second guard should come at you from the middle of the complex. He's the demo expert's personal bodyguard and shouldn't prove a huge threat if you expect him. The demo expert is planting the demo charge at about this time. He works on the columns right at the heart of the complex, just to the east of where you'll encounter his bodyguard. No matter what you do, kill the demo expert fast. You can lay waste to the rest of the terrorists later, but objective #1 isn't complete without a dead demo guy. If you take too long, the charges will detonate and you lose.

After they go down, there's a two-man patrol that paces the far eastern row. If you come at it from the north, you should get at least one clear shot before the enemies return fire. They usually hug the wall. Do the same for protection, or flank out for a better kill shot. With persistence, all nine veteran-level enemies should see their last terrorist mission.

EXPLOSIVE PRISONERS

Four enemies secure the refinery's northwest corner, and they're not happy to see you.

You can relax a little once the demo expert's charges are safely disarmed. Rather than let the enemy escape to haunt you later, clean up the refinery area row by row.

A four-man squad guards the western exit. Its members take cover as soon as they spot you, and one runs across the concourse and tries to flank you from the south. Take cover and get the best angle to expose them the most. You don't want the one in the south to get close for a quality shot, but the other three should be your priority.

Six mercenaries hide in the weeds waiting to gun you down from both sides of the road.

Take the road west out of the refinery. You won't go far. In fact, you can probably shoot the enemies from *inside* the refinery if they show their faces. They like to hide in the weeds, so be careful. There are mercenaries on either side of the road. If you don't count six dead, you missed one.

This pipeline doesn't lead to oil; it leads to a machine gun nest and innocent hostages.

After that firefight, head south toward the pipeline. Swinging under the massive tube, follow the cliff until you come up on the machine gun nest from its northeast side. Though heavily protected, the machine gunner goes down easily. He's watching the road to the southeast, in case your team felt foolhardy.

Approach the machine gun nest from the northeast for a clean shot on the gunner. He's watching the southeast in case you headed up the road from the beach.

Alpha takes out the machine gun nest. Meanwhile, move Bravo down along the building to the northeast of the maintenance garage. Hunker them down for a clear shot at the space in front of the open garage doors. Five guards in total—three by the railroad tracks and two along the pipeline—stand in your way outside the garage. Get Bravo in good enough position so that when Alpha emerges from the machine gun nest to trade rounds with the terrorists, it's lights out for anyone who doesn't know the Pledge of Allegiance.

Five enemy soldiers secure the perimeter of the maintenance garage where the prisoners are held.

With resistance wiped out around the building, enter the makeshift prison. Remember those explosives in the first jeep you encountered? They're all stored in here. One stray bullet and you won't have to worry what they're serving in the mess hall tomorrow. Take all the guards out around the building first so that they don't shoot *into* the building.

Bust in from the open door on the eastern wall. There are two enemies watching the prisoners. One roams in the middle of the crates. The other is hidden to your left. Punch in quick and control your shots to well-aimed, single-fire bursts. The guard to your left is particularly troublesome; he has a great shot at you, especially if you concentrate on the unsuspecting guard in the center of the room.

No one else secures the prisoners, so after the two enemies fall, it's as simple as "running into" each prisoner. If you don't activate them in this way, the workers will sit in the room like obedient puppies waiting for their master to return. Don't leave them behind or you won't complete the second objective.

If you don't want your prisoners charbroiled, watch where you fire your weapons in the garage. Those crates don't hold balloons.

ADVANCED TRAINING

Follow the tracks to freedom.

At this point, you may have a free ride to the extraction zone. If so, take it easy and enjoy a peaceful stroll down the tracks.

If you left any terrorists running around, particularly in the refinery area, they'll double back and try to cut you off at the tracks. You don't want to get in a firefight with the workers in tow. If you fear a fight, keep whoever has the prisoners inside the garage. Switch to the other team and use them to clear a path to the extraction zone. One way or another, you'll track them down.

The end of the line means another job well done.

Because of the time limit at the beginning of the mission, you might have to restart this one a few times to get it right. If you complete it in one pass without any casualties, hotshot, give yourself a medal and try the next mission with your eyes closed.

DS MISSION 3: COLD STEAM

Trains, surface-to-air missile launchers, and secret documents—what more could you ask from a mission? Like the previous mission, this one puts you on the clock. The second you start shooting bad guys in the main area, the train yard, the head bad guys smarten up and try to beat feet with the secret docs. Can you mow down two dozen mercenaries and retrieve the intelligence papers in time?

LEGEND

- **①** **Number of Enemies at Location**
- **①** **Objective Number**
- **●** **Stop Points**
- **▪** **Insertion Zone**

MISSION CONDITIONS

Mission Name:	*DS M3 Cold Steam*
Location:	*Southern Denakil Awraja, Eritrea*
Date:	*05/29/09*
Time:	*15:30*
Weather:	*Sunny*
Item Requirements:	*M136 Rocket Launcher*

OBJECTIVES

1. *Eliminate Mobile SAM Launcher*
2. *Neutralize Tent Camp*
3. *Secure Depot Buildings*
X. *Capture Intelligence Items*

UPHILL BATTLE

You start the mission on top of the northeast hill and need to battle two patrols before you head to the train station. Run to the where your plateau slopes down to the next level and you can survey the entire area. The first three-man patrol is on your left. They stick together, so you can spray the group and take them all down in seconds. If you miss, they seek cover behind the trees. You must then flank out to get a shot around the trunks.

The first three-man patrol won't know what hit them.

The next patrol is in one of two places: either down another level on the next plateau or *right on top of you*. Depending on how much time you take with the first group, the second four-man enemy team might reinforce. Be prepared to gun the four down from your current position or head down to the next plateau and use the rocks for cover as you pick them off.

The second patrol might reinforce its friends after the shooting starts.

BOXCARS AND BULLETS

Catch the guards walking the train hangar unaware by cutting around to the back doors.

Stick to the train hangar's eastern hill for cover as you head down to tackle the main mercenary force. If you go toward the north side of the hangar, you'll walk into a crossfire. Use the south end (the one with the deserted car parked out in the field) to sneak around and surprise the three-man team inside.

Two guards charge at you from the small train booth.

Advance and shoot inside the hangar. Don't give the enemy a chance to return fire. If you're having trouble—say, the enemy's entrenched in good defensive positions—there's a "secret passage" corridor that runs under the trains, which you can navigate for a surprise attack.

TIP

During the mission, keep your demolitions expert safe so he can load up his M136 at the end of the mission.

Once you get to the northern end, two enemies charge at you from the small booth directly ahead. They try to close for better shots, so take them out with your longer-range M16s. Don't push forward past the bay doors or you'll contend with a four-man mercenary team trying to pop you from the train yard.

Advance too far, and the enemy will ambush you from around the side of the hangar.

One note with the train yard: Those with the better cover will win. You have the element of surprise, which means you'll catch your enemies out in the open more times than not. Shoot quickly before they can dive behind barrels, boxcars, and barricades. Stay within the hangar, especially alongside the train, and you cut down on the number of enemies that can see and shoot at you. They also can't get a good angle on you for an exposed shot.

Having trouble with guards in the train hangar? Use the "secret passage" under the parked train to take them by surprise.

There should be one last patrol in the train yard, and it's the toughest. It guards the far side of the yard. After the shooting breaks out, the three enemies take fortified positions along the third set of train tracks. From there, they don't come out. Expect heavy resistance as they fire from under the train and alongside the cars.

The enemy fires from underneath the trains to maximize cover.

Eventually, you have to pry those three enemies out of there to complete objective #3. The catch is that you have to do all this on a time clock. Take too long and the top secret intelligence files will be gone. Once the bigwigs hear the gunfire, they're heading for the hills. If you think the fight by the hangar has taken too long, give up on the three holed-up enemies. Set team Bravo up inside the hangar, and run Alpha toward the special objective. You can always take the last three train yard enemies down later—you can't retrieve the secret papers later.

SECRET FILES

Cut between the railroad cars, past the water tower, to the two buildings next to the tracks. These hold the secret documents.

Dash quickly past the railroad cars and run up the porch of either of the intelligence buildings. It doesn't matter which one you tackle first. Head to the gray door, open it, and get in position to move upstairs. You have to be fast here. One enemy might be exposed at the top of the stairs. Shoot him and continue firing while moving up the stairs. It's kill or be killed. Don't miss or you'll be a new wall decoration.

CAUTION

The enemies inside the intelligence buildings have superior positioning. Stay under the second-story balcony, or they'll shoot you from above.

Three well-armed enemies hold the first half of the secret documents.

Take the same approach with the second group of intelligence enemies as you did with the first. If the special objective window doesn't show up when you kill the last enemy, zigzag around the second story a bit to trigger the objective condition.

You complete the special objective when you eliminate the second three-man team in the intelligence building.

If you left the last three enemies to pursue the escaping documents, you can now catch them in a crossfire. Before you leave the intelligence building, toggle back to team Bravo. Peek out of the hangar till you can see one of the enemies, drop prone, and rip off a few shots. You want to catch their attention.

Switch back to Alpha and charge out of the intelligence building. Bravo draws the fire from the remaining enemies, and they should have their backs to you. You can't ask for easier targets.

FLANKS A LOT

Sneak up on the tent encampment from its northern hill.

Your last big push takes you south to the enemy tent encampment. It's an easy approach. There's really only one way to attack—from the tent's northern hill. If you come up slowly, your sight at full range, you'll have a clean shot at two enemies in the center of camp. Hit at least one, then flank the camp to your right. At the gaps between the tent, fire at any exposed enemies, then slide to the next gap. Keep Bravo at the point where you shot the first tent enemy. If any enemy uses the middle of the camp as an escape route or tries to outflank you, Bravo will teach him a lesson.

Some enemies are just plain stubborn. You might have to weave through the tent obstacles to get a clear shot. Dodge from crate to chair and pick off where you can, even if just an elbow or leg is showing on the bad guy. Usually, the best option is patience. Eventually, the enemy has to move into an arc of fire if you have him surrounded.

After you open fire on the first guards, don't stop. Continue moving to your right and shoot any guard who moves.

SAM SLAM

To wipe out the surface-to-air missile launcher, you must first take out the two guards.

From the tent encampment, head up the road to the east—it takes you right to the SAM site. Hug the rocks to avoid being spotted. There are only two guards watching the SAM, and their attention is on the north, where they overlook the train yard.

If you want to play it safe, switch to someone other than your demo expert and clip the first guard. The second guard should come back over the rise to investigate. You're faster than he is, so this fight shouldn't be much of a strain.

One M136 antitank rocket blows apart the SAM.

As the coup de grace, switch to your demo expert and load up an antitank rocket. One missile should do the trick. Without the SAM, your air strikes can finally bomb the enemy supply lines and send the bad guys scurrying back to their holes like rats.

DS MISSION 4: QUIET ANGEL

Remember back in mission 10, when you had to run shotgun for a bunch of tanks through the blasted street of Vilnius? It's time to do it again, desert-style. This time you have to protect a truck caravan, the bad guys use sand dunes instead of street rubble, and you have to take elevation into account. The only two constants are that you have to hustle to intercept the enemy, and the mercenaries have again gotten ahold of the latest, high-tech rocket launchers to flatten your allied trucks.

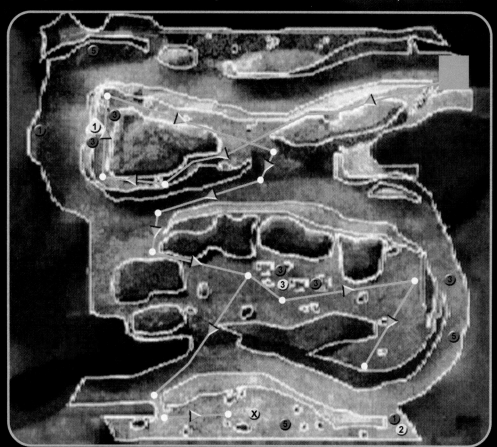

LEGEND

- **① Number of Enemies at Location**
- **① Objective Number**
- **● Stop Points**
- **■ Insertion Zone**

MISSION CONDITIONS

Mission Name:	*DS M4 Quiet Angel*
Location:	*Tigray Kilil, Ethiopia*
Date:	*06/04/09*
Time:	*16:00*
Weather:	*Sunny*
Item Requirements:	*M136 Rocket Launcher*

OBJECTIVES

1. *Secure Rocket Launcher Site 1*
2. *Secure Rocket Launcher Site 2*
3. *Defend all Friendly Trucks*
X. *Eliminate all Enemy Units*

NO SNIPERS

Riflemen, not snipers, should safeguard the allied truck convoy.

For this mission, you break your cardinal rule that the sniper is the most important soldier type. You can still take one for long-range hits, but no more than that. You need the closer firefight ability of riflemen for the point-blank combat you're bound to run into. Also, you don't have time to line up a shot by the sniper. If you delay, the enemy will engage and overrun your trucks while you're not looking after them.

TIP

This isn't a mission of stealth. Consequently, you're going to leave your snipers at home.

ROCKET LAUNCHER #1

At the northwest plateau, take the left fork around the divide to ambush the enemy from the protection of the rocks.

Run from the start. You don't have time to sit around. You might think it's best to follow the truck caravan and shoot anything that moves; it's not. If you try that, the enemy will have elevation on you and much better cover to ambush you. Instead, head up the hill to your left and fight for the high ground.

At the top of the plateau, head west and bear left when you hit the rocky divide. Approach from the southern side, there's more cover and you've got a good chance of surprising the enemy. When you near the western edge, slide around the corner and identify where the six-man team patrols.

Six enemies wait for your truck convoy on the northwest plateau. You don't have much time to waste, so hit them with everything you've got.

You have to hurry. Your truck convoy, which you've temporarily abandoned, should be halfway down the northern corridor at this point. When the convoy gets to the northwest corner, you have to be there to support it, so don't waste time in a long firefight. Swing out so all three of your teammates can shoot the unsuspecting enemies.

A lone enemy with a rocket launcher hides on the western wall to end your mission prematurely.

When the last of the plateau troops falls, the objective #1 menu pops up. It's a lie. The rocket launcher enemy is still out there, and he'll kill your trucks if you relax even for a second. Reload on the run, then head to the western cliff, halfway down the western corridor where the objective #1 symbol is on the map. Use your zoom to search the far side cliff face. A small figure is hidden on the cliff wall. He's got the rocket launcher and plans to use it. Pick him off, then move to the northwest corner of the plateau.

CAUTION

The hardest part of the mission is your first few battles. You must eliminate the objective #1 enemies before a second group of guards ambushes the truck convoy on the road.

Five enemies look to kill your truck drivers from in close.

If you time everything right, you arrive as your truck convoy reaches the map's northwest section. Five enemies try to swarm the truck convoy and barrage your drivers with bullets. From your vantage point, you have clear shots at the enemies. It shouldn't take more than a few seconds to clear them out.

TOWER RUINS

Cut through this small access point to get a jump on the largest enemy group.

You have a little more time now that you've dealt with the first rocket launcher threat. Head south for the center of the map. When you reach the center plateau, head west and hug the cliffs until you find a small crack through the walls. This cuts to the top of the plateau and puts you behind the enemy soldiers. It's the best approach. If you head around to the other side, you'd face the muzzle of a machine gun at point-blank range.

Take the broken tower guards from behind to minimize your casualties.

Before you tackle the broken tower guards, call up your mission map and set coordinates for team Bravo to advance on the north side of the ruins. When Bravo begins its move, charge Alpha at the enemies' backs. With accurate shots, you'll take out four of the six enemies by the broken tower without a shot in your direction. Have Alpha rain a bunch of shots between the ruined walls, then flank to the right. Bravo's shots pick off anyone you (as Alpha) can't see. When you get an unobstructed shot, blast the last enemy in the makeshift machine gun nest in the tower. The trickiest part of this firefight is not shooting your teammates as you flank from opposite directions.

Flank the enemies hiding behind the ruins and in the machine gun bunker.

ROCKET LAUNCHER #2

The first of two enemy patrols in the east corridor doesn't see you coming from above.

The middle of the map should be cleared by now. Head east until you reach the cliffs, then scan the eastern corridor. Directly below you is a three-man team hoping to engage your truck convoy as it rounds the corner. With the advantage from above, unload on the unsuspecting enemies, and send them to an early grave.

The second enemy group in the east corridor is a feisty lot that returns serious fire.

Farther south on the eastern corridor, a second team of five enemies lies in wait. These guys are much more efficient. You may take out one or two, but they're fast and break apart to avoid gunfire spreads and grenades. If you see too many gunfire streaks whizzing by your head, drop prone at the edge to give yourself more cover. Unless the convoy is on top of you, don't take unnecessary chances. Don't move on until these five are dead.

Up on a ramp in the southeast corner, the last rocket launcher enemy looks to surprise your truck convoy.

The most important enemy in this map section is the guy with the rocket launcher. You can wipe out the first three-man team, then the second five-man team, but if you miss this enemy, you lose. He stands on the ramp in the map's southeast corner. If the truck convoy gets as close as the southern half of the eastern corridor, he can light it up. Avoid this scene with a couple of well-placed bullets in his direction.

THE LAST MILE

This is as far as your truck convoy gets if you don't take out that second rocket launcher.

You're almost home free. The southern corridor doesn't have any enemies left. The truck convoy approaches methodically, and you can guide it toward the extraction zone. One enemy patrol is still on the map. They're wandering on the southern-most plateau, looking for a good position to whack you. It's possible to get the convoy out without engaging these enemies.

To be safe, send one of your teams up the ramp in the south-west corner. Be alert. Depending on where the enemy patrol is in its route, you could run into it head on. Hopefully, you can catch it from behind and make it a massacre. If the enemies become aware of you, use local rocks as cover and return fire. Killing them is a bonus; you really just want to tie them up so they can't stop the caravan.

A five-man patrol scours the southern-most plateau for signs of your approaching truck convoy.

When the last of the truck convoy hits the extraction zone, know that you've done a good deed. The trucks are filled with food for the starving refugees in the Denakil desert, and you've prevented the local warlords from stealing the goods. You've saved lives—just make sure you save your own the next time you run into the warlords' men.

DS MISSION 5: GAMMA DAWN

A downed plane, the high-speed reconnaissance Aurora, has gone down in a riverbed a mile from an enemy base. While it's in their backyard, the bad guys can steal your top-secret technology and sell it to the highest bidder. The mission is to destroy the three parts of the downed plane and eliminate the enemy base so no one escapes with your secrets.

LEGEND

- **1** **Number of Enemies at Location**
- **1** **Objective Number**
- ● **Stop Points**
- ■ **Extraction Zone**
- ■ **Insertion Zone**

MISSION CONDITIONS

Mission Name:	*DS M5 Gamma Dawn*
Location:	*Denakil Desert, Ethiopia*
Date:	*06/11/09*
Time:	*23:00*
Weather:	*Clear (Night)*
Item Requirements:	*Demo Charge*

OBJECTIVES

1. *Place Demo Charges at Crash Sites*
2. *Secure Enemy Base*
3. *Reach Extraction Zone*
X. *Secure Supply Depot*

TIP

Take two demolitions experts on this mission so you don't run out of charges to destroy the three pieces of Aurora debris.

DOWNED BIRD

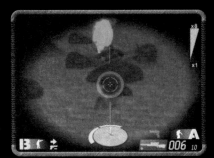

Destroying the downed reconnaissance aircraft.

You start on top of the bridge. If you head up the road, you'll run into the enemy. Instead, switch to your sniper and walk to the lip of the cliff. Drop prone and survey the territory.

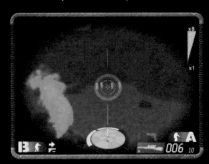

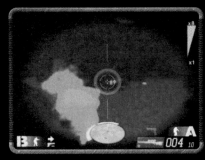

A five-man enemy team guards the second piece of the Aurora.

Down in the riverbed, a five-man team guards the broken Aurora plane. The enemies are walking around the second piece—the one with smoke billowing out of it. Zoom in with your sniper scope and take them out one-by-one. Start with the enemy on the left. After you fire your first shot, the enemies try to take cover. You don't want any of them to move to your left, or else they'll disappear into the smoke and make it difficult to pick them off.

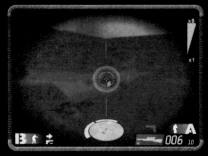

The third piece of the Aurora craft is on the northern cliff face.

Swing up on the cliff face on the other side of the riverbed, directly across from your position. That's the third piece of the Aurora, and two enemies are stripping it down for parts and useable technology. Because of your angle, you can only see one of the two. Take care of the other one when you climb the path up to the third piece. Shoot the one you can see, then swing left for your last set of targets.

Two guards protect the straight-on approach up the road.

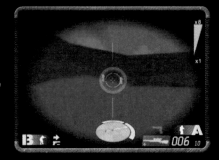

Two guards watch the main road. Shoot them both. If you miss, they'll retreat and warn the rest of the base that someone's attacking. Start with the enemy on the right (the farthest one, and the one closest to the enemy base). When they both fall, switch to a rifleman or demolitions expert and head into the riverbed.

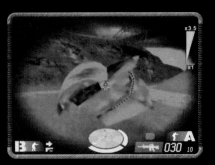

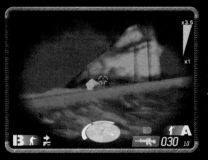

Plant the third demo charge on the last Aurora piece to complete objective #1.

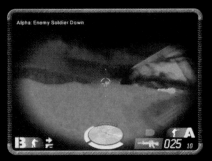

The first two pieces of the Aurora are embedded below the bridge.

There are three pieces of the destroyed plane, but only two of them are in the riverbed. The third lies on the hill to the northeast (see the objective points on the map). Set your first two demo charges here, then move up the path that cuts through the northern face.

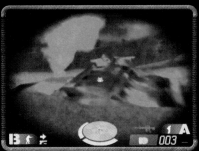

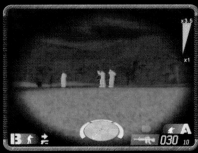

Watch for the two enemies examining the third Aurora piece. Backing them up is a three-man team to the north.

If your sniper did his part, one of the two enemies by the third Aurora piece is dead. On the far side, watch for the second guard and shoot when he's exposed. Another three-man patrol combs the flats north of your position. Wait for the enemies to come into your sites, then mow them down. Make sure that both Alpha and Bravo are set up here so you get more lead flying at the enemy.

SUPPLY DEPOT

Two men guard the depot, and a third comes via truck.

Rather than taking on the enemy base, your special objective, the supply depot, is your next target. Two enemies hang out near the depot, while a third arrives by truck. It takes the guard in the truck a second to orient himself, so hit the two armed guards first.

After the truck driver goes down, wait to charge the supply depot. Look east to spot two enemies itching to plug you should you cut across the open field. Until you clip both those enemies, you can't advance on the depot.

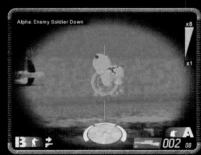

Two enemies try to hit you from behind when you attack the depot. Scan to your right, up the east road, and lock on to them before you move forward.

Three enemies are inside the depot. With such close quarters, it would be difficult to take them out in a fair fight, but you don't have to play fair. Move around to the building's eastern face and inch forward until you see multiple enemies through the window. Switch your rifleman's weapon to the M203 Grenade Launcher and zip one in the enemy's midst. Watch your screen for three enemy kills to appear. If only one or two show up, launch another grenade in there.

Take out the three inside the depot with a grenade through the window.

The last enemy is around the back of the supply depot. He's heard the gunshots and explosions, so he's prepared to take at least one of your team with him. Cut around the corner and drop him.

When you think you've got everything secured, there's still one last enemy behind the depot.

ENEMY BASE

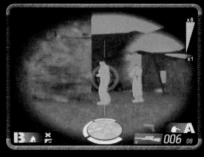

Pick off as many of the enemy as you can in the base's backyard.

Switch to your sniper and, from the safety of the supply depot, scan the enemy base to your west. At least two enemies are inside the complex. Snipe them while you have a chance—no sense running into them later.

Beware of the three enemies on the main road.

As you approach the base from the east, you'll see a three-man patrol in front. One soldier is tending the jeep, and the other two walk farther behind him. These three are dangerous. If you don't eliminate them now, they will wound members of your team later. Prevent that situation from occurring.

Your main goal before moving into the enemy fortress is to eliminate the tower guards. If you don't, they will kill several of your men from their superior vantage points.

Your priority with the sniper is to take down both tower guards. They can see the whole base, and if left alone, they'll rain down heavy fire on your soldiers. It helps to think of this as a reverse prison break—you're breaking in. In any good prison break, you have to eliminate the tower guards or silence them in order to make it past the walls.

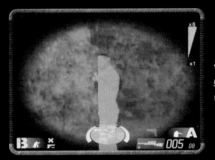

Several of the base guards hide behind walls and rubble.

Inside the compound, there are three or four guards left; they're aware of your presence, so proceed with caution. To your right, the enemies use the building walls as cover; to the left, they hide behind the rubble. Have Alpha take up a defensive position, then call Bravo in toward the building in the backyard. When the enemies pop up to take out Bravo, blast them.

The last two enemies inside the base hide out in the main house.

The commanding officers have retreated to the main house. One waits to blast you when you open the front door. The other hides in the second doorway to your right. Arm yourself with the quickest firing weapon. Whoever draws and hits first wins.

HOMEWARD BOUND

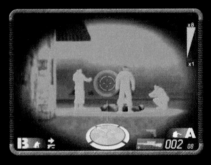

Only one enemy group remains in the village on your return trip to the extraction zone.

Return to the extraction zone, which was the insertion zone earlier. A three-man team is hanging out around a campfire in the village. If you approach from the north, they won't see you coming. Creep in till you line one of them up with the perfect shot. Take that enemy down, then move on to the other two.

With the whole enemy base dead, your bosses don't have to worry about information leaking into foreign hands. Good work—this was your last night mission of the campaign.

DS MISSION 6: SPECTRE WIND

The Ghosts are about to enter a ghost town. The local warlord, Ashenafi Abate, has set up a stronghold in a deserted town outside Adi K'eyih. Abate has laid landmines all over the place, and it's your job to recover his minefield maps and pry Abate out of his fortress. Along the way, you'll need to neutralize Abate's vehicle pool, which includes a stolen tank. Bring extra ammo because you're about to enter the firefight to end all firefights.

MISSION CONDITIONS

Mission Name: *DS M6 Spectre Wind*

Location: *Adi K'eyih, Eritrea*

Date: *06/16/09*

OBJECTIVES

1. *Retrieve Map of Minefields*

2. *Neutralize Vehicle Pool*

3. *Capture Warlord*

THE FIREFIGHT

Two machine gun nests will cut you down if you're not careful.

Before you enter the town, you've engaged 20 enemies. Your first few minutes in the ghost town are a bloodbath. After you fire your first shot, hunker down and prepare for a lot of different minibattles as Abate's soldiers reinforce the besieged village guards.

To start, take one of your snipers to the last rock before you head into town. As usual, go prone and scan the area. Up on the fortress hill, two machine gun nests aim at you. These should go first; you don't want machine gun fire raining down on your fireteams.

The village guards advance on your position unless you dissuade them with heavy fire.

Six enemies patrol the middle of the village. When you fire on the nests, they charge at you. Unless you want to quit early, you need to fire into their midst and send them dashing for cover. Most of them hide behind the trees and structures below the machine gun nests. Don't move yet. You can take each one of them out if you have patience.

When the enemy breaks up, scan from tree to tent to find them.

There are a lot of reinforcements. Three jeeps show up on the scene with an armed guard each. If you can take out a driver while his jeep is in motion, it will explode and do some additional damage to those around it. If you can't, then catch a guard as he exits a jeep. Each guard hesitates for a moment at the driver's side door while grabbing his weapon. The guards are vulnerable at that time.

Three jeeps show up with reinforcements for the village guards.

Besides the jeeps, other soldiers abandon their posts to help out. Expect two to four more guards to show up in the area *after* you've "cleared" it out. Always keep on your toes when crossing through the village. One bullet can end your mission.

GRABBING THE MAPS

A three-man patrol tries to ambush you from the paths networking to the north of the village.

After the big firefight in town, double back to the northeast and cut up the dirt path that leads into the northern hills. Three enemies approach from that direction, hoping to surprise you from above. You may not see them right away, as the hill slopes steeply up, but they are on the other side. Shoot those three, and your path is clear to the building with the minefield documents.

Four guards surround the building with the minefield papers.

Approach the minefield building from the north. You have plenty of rock cover to get there undetected. Cut through the gap between the rocks and the nearest building, then surprise the guards in front of the minefield building. A four-man team guards the outside, and its members usually stay spread out. Take out the two by the door, then scan around for the other two. One comes from behind the building a few seconds after you start shooting.

Shoot the enemy guarding the minefield papers through the window. Otherwise, you'll have a difficult time killing him sneaking in through the doorway.

If you move too far into the open space, the enemy inside the minefield building will join in. He fires at you through his office window (to the left of the door), so return the favor with some projectiles aimed at his head. Pick him off through the window. It's easier than sneaking in the door and turning the corner to face a point-blank shot.

After the minefield documents are recovered, use your sniper to search out any enemy stragglers who may harass you on your return trip.

TIP

Until you seize Abate in his house, you never have to leave the hills where you started. The rest of the enemies can be shot from the safety of the rocks.

With objective #1 complete, double back the way you came, and head toward the vehicle pool on the map's southwest section. Search for any enemy interference in the village—another reinforcement jeep or more unaccounted for guards—and deal with them immediately. It's easy to lose track of the enemies' positions on this mission, and that's a surefire way of getting shot.

On the way to the vehicle pool, pick off Abate's guards to save on work later.

JUNKYARD ARTILLERY

Six of Abate's men protect his prized possession, a tank.

The vehicle pool soldiers are expecting an attack from the main road. Two snipers lay prone in the middle of the junkyard, itching to trigger a few at the first commandos they see. One of the guards mans a machine gun for extra firepower, but the hill paths lead behind the junkyard and set you up for the perfect ambush.

A machine gun and two snipers lying prone on the ground point toward the east and the main road, so attack from the north.

If your sniper has any leftover ammo, track down as many enemies as you can, and pick them off. The two snipers are easy targets, as is the lone guard standing in the junkyard's center. One guard hangs out near the cliffs beneath you; he's the toughest to hit. He has the element of cover between the rocks and the vehicles. However, he can't get a good shot at you without popping up, so time your shot for his movement.

Two more guards patrol the back of the vehicle pool. Before you fight them one on one, have your demolitions soldier break out his M136 and launch a missile at the tank. The explosion may kill the two remaining guards. If not, grab a rifleman and go down the path into the junkyard and look for the guards between the debris.

Your demo expert needs to launch an antitank missile into the armored unit on the junkyard's far side.

THE FORTRESS

Abate has five guards entrenched as perimeter defense, most of them behind sandbag barriers.

From the junkyard, cut across the road and charge up the hill at Abate's house. There is little resistance now. At the house's southwest corner, slide out and draw a bead on the enemy by the sandbags. His partner is by the tree to the left, so proceed cautiously until the perimeter is clear.

Even though Abate shoots at you, if you kill him, you lose the mission. Shoot the guard to his right (in camouflage) to end the firefight.

Your last task is to retrieve Abate. He has only one guard, and you've surrounded them, but they are armed and ready for you when you come through the door. The problem is telling which one is Abate. It doesn't matter if Abate shoots you; if you shoot him, the mission ends in failure. You could kill everyone else in the mission, but one slip of the finger and it's over.

The prize, Ashenafi Abate, gives up after all his men are dead.

The answer to your dilemma is to shoot Abate's guard. The guard is to the right, dressed in camouflage. He also has a slighter build than Abate. When the guard drops, Abate gives up, and you've completed the mission. Count yourself lucky if no one on your team was killed by Abate's men. More bullets fly on this mission than any other in the game.

DS MISSION 7: SUBTLE KEEP

The bad guys have finally got the hang of things by the second-to-last mission. While you may take two snipers on your team, they wield six against you on the first part of your new mission. Outgun them, and go through another 14 soldiers in a fortified position. Should you survive that death run, your last challenge is to take a keep surrounded by hidden traps and invisible enemies. No problem, right?

LEGEND

- ① **Number of Enemies at Location**
- ① **Objective Number**
- ● **Stop Points**
- ▪ **Extraction Zone**
- ▪ **Insertion Zone**

MISSION CONDITIONS

Mission Name:	*DS M7 Subtle Keep*
Location:	*Akale Guzay Awraja, Eritrea*
Date:	*06/22/09*
Time:	*16:00*
Weather:	*Sunny*
Item Requirements:	*None*

OBJECTIVES

1. *Neutralize Roadblock and Snipers*
2. *Secure Compound*
3. *Neutralize all Enemy Vehicles*
X. *Reach Extraction Zone*

SNIPER ALLEY

The first of three snipers waits for you in a cement bunker above the road.

All seems quiet on the main road, and that's what the enemy wants you to think. Of course, it's a trap. Snipers line the cliff walls in cement bunkers on the hills. Three snipers aim at you from the first northeast hill, with another opposite them on the far side of the road. Unlike regular soldiers, these snipers can strike you from long range. They might use the same high-powered weapons as your snipers.

 TIP

Arm your sniper with a 7.62mm sniper rifle or the M98 for scopes with 12x or better range.

Don't go down the road. The snipers will pick apart your team, and you'll have to restart. Instead, hug the cliff wall for maximum cover and get into a position to view all the bunkers and snipe their snipers. With the 7.62mm sniper rifle or the M98, focus inside the bunkers and line up kill shot after kill shot.

On the other side of the road, another sniper shoots at you.

After you thwart the first set of sniper crossfires, run your sniper up the hill where the bunkers are to line up your next set of shots. The second sniper zone has two snipers; however, if you delay, some enemies may find their way up the hills and cause you problems. Take out the last sniper, then move to the sniper bunkers for a clear view of the roadblock you've been sent to destroy.

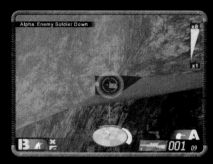

On the last hill before the roadblock, a final sniper can ruin your day.

ROAD RAGE

Fourteen guards clog the road near the blockade.

Your sniper's got more work cut out for him. No matter how good your riflemen and support soldiers are, they can't get through the roadblock without assistance. The enemy has the benefit of cover and superior numbers. Your teams would be ripped apart as they advanced down the open road.

First, take out the five-man team to your right. You don't want them gaining the hill and firing at you from a higher elevation. Next, swing over to the three-man team on the left.

The sniper whittles down the resistance before you go in. Zoom in on the five-man team to the right. You want its members dead so they can't climb the hill and shoot at you from above. As they fall, pan across the road and pick off anyone you can pinpoint. Your last targets should be in the three-man team to your left.

Two jeeps reinforce the roadblock, but a shot to the gas tank singes that extra soldier.

Two jeeps show up to reinforce the blockade. Unfortunately for the drivers, they're operating vehicles with enormous gas tanks. One shot to the jeep sparks the gas tank, and the whole jeep explodes.

If you can get close to the roadblock, unload on the guards hiding behind the vehicles as quickly as you can.

Your sniper can single-handedly kill the roadblock soldiers. If you're fast and your cover gets in the way of incoming shots, the entire roadblock area can be cleared without risk to your other five soldiers. Wait for everyone stops moving, then send your troops down on the road. To make an accurate determination, pull back on your zoom to take in the whole area.

Watch out for the assassin lying along the cliff base near the main road's southeast intersection.

HOUSE ON THE HILL

The house at the bottom of the keep's hill hosts three enemies who guard the road.

Leg three of your journey takes you to the keep on the hill. At the bottom of the hill, three soldiers patrol the road. Don't be fooled if no one's around when you arrive. The three-man patrol walks back and forth between the road and the back of the small house adjacent to the road. Wait for all three to expose themselves before you open up.

The ominous-looking keep is your last objective.

The hill looks like a difficult assault, and it is. Other than the big rock halfway up the hill, there isn't much cover. On top of that, the enemies have built a series of trenches around the keep to give them hiding places to lie in wait. It's a trap, and you have to disarm it.

Don't get caught in control of your sniper when you advance on the keep's hill. The enemy will quickly gun you down.

Switch off your sniper. The battles from here on out are close and quick. Better that you control a rifleman or support soldier for the firefights.

Like a moat, the enemy has dug a trench system around the keep from which assassins can pop up and wipe you out.

Run for the cover of the big rock and drop prone if anyone fires at you. Watch out for the machine gun near the southeast part of the trench system. Unless a patrol wanders down the hill, there is only one enemy on the southeast perimeter, near the machine gun. Kill that enemy and jump into the trench.

Near the trench system, machine guns stand ready for the enemy to use at any time.

TIP

Use the enemies' trench system against them. It keeps you hidden from anyone outside the trenches and acts like a road map—follow the trenches to find all the enemies.

Now you're on equal footing with the protected enemies. Follow the trench system in a clockwise fashion. On the western face, a three-man team intercepts you around the southwest corner. At the top of the hill, behind the keep, another three-man team stakes out the trenches. These guys are tougher and have access to a machine gun, and have been forewarned that you're coming. If you can finish them off, one more enemy is on the northeast perimeter. There are eight total ringing the keep.

At the top of the hill, behind the keep, three of the enemies shoot at you as you round either of the keep's corners.

There are only two enemies left at this point. If you're on the keep's north face, locate a door near the northwest corner. Monitor this door at all times. One of the enemies likes to kick it open and come out firing. If you have your back turned when he makes his move, you're toast. Wait for the door to spring open, and catch him by surprise when he surfaces.

Two enemies hide inside the keep and use the back door to sneak up on you.

The final enemy hides out inside the keep. You can snipe him from either of the keep's doorways, or send a soldier in to end the mission. Be careful and you'll come away without a scratch. If you've missed anyone, don't worry about it. Command has given you the night off, and they're sending in another platoon to clean up any stragglers. Finally, someone appreciates your efforts.

DS MISSION 8: TORN BANNER

It's Colonel Wolde's last hurrah. He plans on driving his remaining tanks into the field in a last-ditch effort to rally the troops. Your mission is to destroy both river crossing points—a soldier-held ford and a strategically located bridge— then go after Colonel Wolde and his three tanks. Bring lots of rockets if you want to succeed.

LEGEND

- **Number of Enemies at Location**
- **Objective Number**
- **Stop Points**
- **Insertion Zone**
- **Tank**

MISSION CONDITIONS

Mission Name: *DS M8 Torn Banner*

Location: *Mereb Wenz crossing, near Adi*

Date: *06/25/09*

Time: *11:00*

Weather: *Sunny*

Item Requirements: *M136 Rocket Launcher*

OBJECTIVES

1. *Secure Secondary Crossing*
2. *Neutralize Mobile SAM Launcher*
3. *Stop Tank Column*
X. *Neutralize Bridge Sefenders*

FORD EXPLORER

Three soldiers patrol the perimeter of the ford—with three more as backup. They're your first targets.

Your first objective is the last stop for Wolde's tanks, if it comes to that. The northeastern ford, lightly guarded by the enemy, serves as a warm-up exercise for the upcoming slugfest against the tanks. Don't take any wounds in the initial fight; you need all your guys healthy for the rest of the mission.

Two backups arrive in trucks when the fighting begins.

Begin with your sniper. Advance to the clump of foliage in front of the insertion zone and scope the enemy from that position. Zoom around till you find all three enemies in your frame. Shoot one, then another, in rapid succession, then track where the remaining enemies duck for cover. Aim for a piece of the enemy that's showing outside the cover. If you can't get a clear shot, move around until you get the proper angle for a kill shot.

Two backups arrive in trucks. They don't pose much threat. If you spot them early, you can hit them inside the truck or just as they exit the vehicle. Don't let them run from the vehicle or they'll reinforce from a defensive position and be that much tougher to remove.

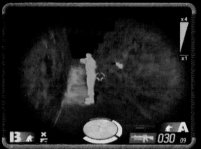

Sneak into the house by the ford to take care of the three guards inside.

Three guards shoot at you from the boarded-up house on the hill by the ford. When the ford guards are down, run for the house and skirt around to the north face. Find the back door and enter with a rifleman. One guard tries to take you at the first doorway, so shoot as you round the corner. A second guard emerges from the first doorway on your right. The last guard stays in his room down on the right. Be careful with him; he's armed with a machine gun and doesn't miss often.

After you've dealt with the ford, toggle to your other team (Bravo) at the insertion zone, and head south into the rocks. Usually, on the western side of the big rock shielding the insertion zone from the rest of the map, three enemies look to reinforce whenever they get a chance. Their favorite trick is to come up behind you after you've "cleared" a zone. Don't give them the chance. Hunt the three enemies down and pick them off before they do damage.

With the three enemies down, send Bravo to the cliffs on the map's southern end. Get in position to overlook the road leading to the small bridge. Alpha plays an important role later when the tanks roll in on you.

ARMOR HILL

The first machine gun nest on the hill guards the SAM behind it.

Outside the house, toggle back to your sniper and scout up the hill. On the other side of the rocky tip, locate the first of two machine gun nests. They flank the SAM you've been assigned to take out (objective #2). Watching through your scope, when you top the ridge, line up a good shot and eliminate the guard in the nest.

Switch back to a rifleman and charge up to the rocks. There are four enemies left, one in the second machine gun nest. Take the guard out in the nest, then move on to the others. Hopefully your superior cover can protect you, but it's a tough fight.

Five enemies ring the SAM and try to buy time for their tank division to rumble to the rescue.

When the bad guys are dead, switch to your demolitions expert and destroy the SAM. For this mission you should have two demo experts, both with M136s, and they should be kept out of harm's way until the last fight. Without them, you have no hope against the incoming tanks.

One antitank missile ends the SAM threat.

DEATH OR GLORY

A forward three-man team announces the imminent tank arrival.

You don't have much time now. The tanks are on their way. Switch to a sniper and blast the first few enemies you see. A forward advance of three enemies heralds the tanks' approach. Take them out so your demo expert has an unobstructed view of the tanks. If the tanks crest the rise, switch to your demo guy. If those tanks unload on you, you're finished.

Three missiles, three tanks—if you miss, you're dead.

The fate of your platoon rests on your demolitions expert's shoulders, literally. He has to load up an antitank rocket and hit the first tank as it rises over the ridge. Reload and strike the second tank as it dodges around the first tank's blazing chassis. Repeat for the third tank.

Each time you kill a tank, the others get dangerously closer. You can't miss here. You don't have time to reload and blast a missed tank before it blasts you. Take your time to line up the shot and make sure it's nestled in the center of the tank's body. Don't be intimidated by those big turrets swinging toward your face—your weapon is just as powerful as theirs.

Use the southwestern rope bridge to outflank the bridge guards if necessary.

Click on the map and toggle over to Bravo. Up on the cliffs, look down on the road behind the burning tanks. A second three-man team follows the tank division. It's Bravo's job to take out these soldiers. The enemy is concentrating fire on the demolitions expert who just blew up the tanks. Your demo guy is more than a little handicapped, switching weapons from rocket launcher to M4. You certainly don't want him rewarded with a bullet to the brain after the feat he's just performed, so unload on the exposed enemies below. At the very least, distract them so they turn to fire at you. Eventually, you'll annihilate them from your fortified position.

From the cliffs, Bravo catches the rear tank guard in a crossfire.

The last three soldiers defend the bridge. Not that it matters now that their tanks are blown to smithereens. Even so, they fire back, so have Bravo mow them down from the cliffs. If there's any remaining resistance—maybe one of them lies prone below the concrete side and can't be hit by Bravo—send in Alpha to clean up.

There may be stragglers in the rocks. After the bulk of the work has been accomplished, search for hidden enemies, particularly in the western passages.

After you dispose of the tanks, concentrate your fire on the three enemies defending the bridge.

The mission is not over. Like the team of enemies hiding in the rocks near the insertion zone, there are other enemies hiding near the bridge. There's a stretch of land between the SAM site and the rope bridge that connects to the landmass behind the concrete bridge. Three enemies are entrenched there. They may engage as you take on the tanks, but sometimes your demo expert is so effective that they don't have time to cause harm.

Instead, they wait for you to come to them. You can either bounce from rock to rock on the northern entrance to pick them off, or take the rope bridge and hope to get the jump on them from behind. Either way, they're outgunned and nowhere near as smart as you.

Your African campaign missions are complete. Colonel Wolde has fallen, and you've brought order to the Ethiopian chaos.

Thanks to you, Colonel Wolde's dreams of conquest end up in fiery ruin.